Edinburgh Law E

LEGAL METHOD
ESSENTIALS FOR
SCOTS LAW

EDINBURGH LAW ESSENTIALS

Series Editor: Nicholas Grier, Edinburgh Napier University

Private International Law
David Hill

Revenue Law Essentials
William Craig

Commercial Law Essentials
Malcolm Combe

Succession Law Essentials
Frankie McCarthy

Delict Essentials
Francis McManus

Scottish Legal System Essentials
Bryan Clark and Gerard Keegan

Scottish Evidence Law Essentials
James Chalmers

Contract Law Essential Cases
Tikus Little

Trusts Law Essentials
John Finlay

Company Law Essentials
Josephine Bisacre and Claire
McFadzean

Jurisprudence Essentials
Duncan Spiers

Legal Method Essentials for Scots Law
Dale McFadzean and Lynn Allardyce
Irvine

Human Rights Law Essentials
Valerie Finch and John McGroarty

Planning Law Essentials
Anne-Michelle Slater

Scottish Contract Law Essentials
Tikus Little

Employment Law Essentials
Jenifer Ross

International Law Essentials
John Grant

Media Law Essentials
Douglas Maule and Zhongdong Niu

Intellectual Property Law Essentials
Duncan Spiers

Scottish Family Law
Kenneth Norrie

European Law Essentials
Stephanie Switzer

Roman Law Essentials
Craig Anderson

Property Law Essentials
Duncan Spiers

Medical Law Essentials
Murray Earle

Public Law Essentials
Jean McFadden and Dale McFadzean

Scottish Administrative Law Essentials
Jean McFadden and Dale McFadzean

www.edinburghuniversitypress.com/series/ele

CONTENTS

TABLE OF CASES

TABLE OF STATUTES

1 INTRODUCTION

WHAT IS LAW?

The definitions of law are wide and varied. It has been described by White and Willock as "... the words of someone in authority who has the power to intervene in other people's affairs ... and if they do not comply something unpleasant is liable to befall them", while the Oxford English Dictionary describes law as a "... body of rules, whether proceeding from formal enactment or custom, which a particular state or community recognises as binding on its members or subjects". Law may have many descriptions but it has only one main practical purpose – to restrict and regulate certain kinds of behaviour. The fact that there are laws which most people obey means that you can generally go about your business secure in the knowledge that someone is not going to assault you, or steal your belongings, or generally put your life in danger by failing to take proper care. If someone does carry out this kind of behaviour then the law creates legal consequences. If you commit a crime then you could be fined or sent to prison. If you have injured someone through negligence then you may be forced to pay compensation or damages.

CATEGORISING THE LAW

Public and private law

Scots law deals with many specific subject areas, such as criminal law, the law of contract, and the law of delict, among others. Each of these areas is known as a "branch" of law. For simplicity, each of these branches is further categorised into two distinct groupings: public law and private law. There is no real technical reason for these groupings. It is simply a useful way of categorising the various branches of law under separate headings.

With "public law", the involvement of the state is paramount. Public law relates to the operation of government and the regulation of the relationship between government and citizens. It also regulates other public bodies such as the courts, the Scottish Parliament, local government, and even the police. Key branches of public law include constitutional law, administrative law and criminal law.

On the other hand, with "private law" the involvement of the state is minimal. Instead, private law is more concerned with the regulation of relationships between individual citizens and/or companies and organisations. For example, when a legal relationship between individuals breaks down, such as a contract, this concerns private law. Key branches of private law include contract law, delict and family law.

Civil and criminal law

As well as categorising the various branches of law into both public and private, the law can also be described in terms of civil or criminal. The main difference between civil and criminal law is that a different court structure is used to regulate each. Under criminal law, a special set of criminal courts exists which aims to punish criminal behaviour and impose sanctions on individual liberty. Cases brought before the criminal courts are known as prosecutions and are brought by officials representing the state. In Scotland these are the Procurator Fiscal, the Lord Advocate, or one of their deputies (known as Depute Procurators Fiscal and Advocates Depute). The person against whom the prosecution is brought is called the accused. The standard of proof in a criminal prosecution is "beyond all reasonable doubt". This means that if a jury has a reasonably held doubt, based upon the evidence, as to the accused's guilt, then they must acquit. The standard of proof is set at a high level in order to safeguard the liberty of the accused who may ultimately face imprisonment.

Under civil law, a special set of civil courts exists which deals with disputes arising between two or more parties, where the conduct of one party has caused unjustified loss to another. Such disputes are known as civil cases and when brought before the civil courts they are referred to as "litigation". The person bringing the case to court is known as the pursuer and the person against whom the action is taken is called the defender. Examples of civil cases include a DIY company damaging your home while fitting a new bathroom suite, or a driver running into your vehicle and causing you to suffer from whiplash. In each of these examples, the aggrieved party may attempt to sue the other party before the civil courts if they have failed to fulfil their obligations or pay compensation for any damage caused by their actions. Under the civil law, courts have no power to interfere with individual liberty. Instead of punishment through imprisonment or fine, the civil courts focus upon reparation whereby aggrieved parties are financially recompensed for any loss suffered. As such, the standard of proof is lower than that of the criminal courts and is based upon the "balance of probabilities".

Overlap between civil and criminal law

Often there can be an overlap between the civil and criminal law. This can happen when a type of behaviour occurs which is both criminal and civil in nature. For example, if an individual assaults another person in the street, that individual has committed a crime which can then result in a prosecution taking place before the criminal courts. However, that assault can also be dealt with under the civil law, in that the victim could attempt to sue his assailant for compensation, using the civil courts.

SOURCES OF LAW AND LEGAL RESEARCH

Sources of law

All legal systems must have sources of law. It is these sources which give authority to the rules and principles within any given system. However, the approach to creating and defining these sources will differ according to the type of legal system. Civil law systems, on the whole, are codified. They have been heavily influenced throughout the ages by Roman law and are based upon codified rules and principles logically set out in often encyclopaedic documents. These "codes" are the main source of law.

Common law systems, on the other hand, have developed quite independently of the influence of Roman law. Instead of reliance upon codes as a source of law, they rely upon judicial precedent. As a source of law, precedent consists of the decisions of judges made in cases which are heard before them. From these decisions, legal principles can be drawn from the judges' written decisions which together form a major source of law. Common law systems have been greatly influenced by English law which was little affected by the spread of Roman law.

There is a third type of legal system which is known as the hybrid system. This is the system to which Scots law adheres and it has developed in such a way that it does not conform exclusively to either civil or common law. Instead, it is a mixed system in which one can discern elements of civil or Roman law but also the influence of common law and precedent. This is certainly true of Scotland where, for example, the branch of criminal law is almost wholly derived from common law whereas other branches, such as company law, rely almost entirely on Acts of Parliament which codify them.

Legal research

Effective legal research skills are essential to the study and practice of law. All disciplines and professions require skill sets; however, the nature of law demands particular abilities including being able to address complex legal questions, identify pertinent issues, and find and use appropriate sources of information to address these.

The Quality Assurance Agency (QAA) for Higher Education Subject Benchmark Statement for law (July 2015) defines the academic standards and skills for law graduates. Amongst other things, a law graduate must demonstrate:

> "Ability to conduct self-directed research including accurate identification of issues(s) which require researching, retrieval and evaluation of accurate, current and relevant information from a range of appropriate sources including primary legal sources". (p 7)

All research begins with an identified information gap and need, ie what do you know and what do you need to know? Understanding that is the first step in the process. The next step is to identify appropriate sources of information to answer that research need. Being able to identify appropriate information to answer legal questions requires an understanding of the sources of law and the nature of legal information.

LEGAL INFORMATION: THE SOURCES OF SCOTS LAW

Practising lawyers encounter many types of information. The focus here is on information of most relevance to students of Scots law. This book discusses the structure of legal literature, where and how this can be found, and how it can be used effectively. Methods and tools for finding the law are constantly changing and there is more than one way to access legal information. More information is now available freely online as well as in online subscription services and in traditional print sources. It is really important therefore to be able to distinguish between sources and choose which tool or method will be most appropriate and effective for your particular need.

Primary and secondary sources

Legal literature, or legal information, may be categorised into primary and secondary sources. Primary sources, or formal sources, represent the law itself. Secondary sources contain commentary on, and interpretation of, the law.

Primary sources of Scots law comprise:

- legislation – law made by or under the authority of Parliament;
- case law – law made by judges and decided in court;
- institutional works – codifications of Scots law made between the 17th and 19th centuries;
- custom – traditions not enshrined in either legislation or case law; and
- quasi- or extra-legal sources – codes and guidance issued by public and private bodies.

Secondary sources include:

- textbooks, monographs, research publications;
- journals (or periodicals);
- encyclopaedic works; and
- reference and bibliographic works – including dictionaries, directories, indexes and legal citators.

Other sources

Some additional sources relevant to the study and practice of Scots law deserve consideration:

- Official publications – particularly publications relating to the UK and Scottish Parliaments;
- European Union materials – particularly legislation and case law produced by EU institutions; and
- international and other non-UK legal materials.

Characteristics of legal information

When using legal information you should be aware of its characteristics. You need to consider the information's currency, authority and the jurisdiction to which it relates. Furthermore, there is no single source where you can find all "the law" needed to solve any legal problem. This means that you need to be comfortable using a variety of tools and sources. This is also what makes legal research rewarding.

Currency

One of the principle characteristics of the law is that it constantly changes. New legislation is produced and new cases are decided. This is reflected also in sources of legal information. For this reason it is essential that you are able to find the most up-to-date information. At the same time, some areas of law remain unchanged for long periods and you may need to find law relevant to a time in the past.

You need to know whether the source you have found gives an accurate picture of the law for the period with which you are concerned and, if not, be able to update it. Paying attention to currency is therefore a key consideration when you are handling legal information.

Authority

Some sources of legal information have greater authority than others. This means that where there is more than one source of that specific piece of information, you must pay attention to the authority, ie where the information is from (who created it). Some versions of legislation or specific law reports are regarded as being authoritative. Greater weight may be attached to certain textbooks and journals. In addition, some sources are regarded as official, such as officially published legislation or transcripts of case law.

Jurisdiction

In Scotland it is particularly important to be aware of the jurisdiction to which a source relates. This is because, while some information may be applicable to the UK, many sources contain legal information applicable to either England and Wales or Scotland. Indeed, some sources may relate to non-UK jurisdictions altogether. While non-Scots material is sometimes relevant, it remains important to appreciate the jurisdictional applicability of legal information. This is particularly important if you are using electronic sources of information on a website; you must always be aware of the jurisdiction of the law you are looking at.

No single source

In order to gain an accurate picture of the law in a particular area, you often need to use several sources. A textbook may give an overview of a topic, but you may need to refer to legislation or case law to understand detail, or read a journal article which provides insight into a doubted area of law. Furthermore, you must check that the law you have found is up to date by referring to printed citators or online equivalents.

Print and online sources – which should you use?

Legal information can be found in print and online resources and you may find that you do not always have access to a full range of resources in both formats.

It is common to find sources which are available in both print and online versions. For example, many series of law reports originally produced as printed volumes are available via online database services. It is generally the case that modern case law and legislation are available online. On the other hand, some resources can only be accessed in print form. Many key textbooks on Scots law are still not available electronically though this is gradually changing. Conversely, it is also the case that some resources can only be accessed online and for Government and Parliamentary papers this is increasingly the case.

While online information may be easier to access and is frequently more up to date, it is not necessarily the most appropriate or authoritative source. At the same time, while a leading printed textbook may give a good overview of a subject, it may be out of date and require supplemental online research to update it.

It is therefore not a question of choosing between a print or an online source, rather it is being able to appreciate the validity of a source in itself and its applicability to a particular legal problem. As a legal researcher you will gain expertise in handling a variety of sources in all formats and develop skills for using them effectively. We provide information on useful websites, subscription services and print sources throughout the book.

Essential Facts

- Law can be categorised as either public law or private law. Public law deals with the operation of government and the regulation of the relationship between government and citizens. Private law is concerned with the regulation of relationships between individual citizens and/or companies and organisations.

- The law may be described as civil law or criminal law. The main difference is that each has a different court structure for its regulation. Criminal law deals with the punishment of criminal behaviour while civil law deals with disputes arising between private individuals, where the conduct of one party has caused unjustified loss to another.

- Legal research skills involve: problem identification and analysis; finding appropriate information to solve the problem; and effective communication of the results of analysis and research.

- Legal information is divided into primary and secondary sources. Primary sources represent the law itself. Secondary sources contain commentaries on the law.

- When using legal information, you should be aware of its currency, authority and jurisdiction. There is no single source where you can find all law.
- Sources of legal information can be in print or online formats – you should use both.

Further Reading

- F Grant, *Legal Research Skills for Scots Lawyers* (3rd edn, 2014), Chapter 1.
- P Clinch, *Using a Law Library: a student's guide to legal research skills* (2nd edn, 2001), Chapters 1 and 3.
- J Knowles, *Effective Legal Research* (4th edn, 2016), Chapter 1.
- P Clinch, *Teaching Legal Research* (2nd edn, 2006), Chapter 1.
- R M White, I D Willock and H L MacQueen, *The Scottish Legal System* (5th edn, 2013), Chapter 1.

2 FINDING THE LAW: SOURCES AND TOOLS

As we discussed in the first chapter, as a legal researcher you are likely to use a mix of online and print resources and you may or may not do this in a library. The "law library" remains an important consideration for the legal researcher but you need to think of the library as extending beyond the physical walls of a building. Modern libraries (particularly academic libraries) are much more than physical spaces with physical collections, and banks of computers and desks are just as common as shelves with rows of printed volumes.

Providing access to online services is a core function of a modern library (often called the "library without walls") and is where most of the budget is invested. Online legal databases are an invaluable tool for finding legal information. They make searching intuitive and are usually updated regularly so you can be sure that you are looking at current information. There is also a steep increase in the amount of official information freely accessible online. However, there are important print resources that are essential for the legal researcher to know about. In this chapter we consider some key resources including print, freely accessible websites and online subscription services that make up the "library" of materials of value to you as a legal researcher.

Accessing a law library

Staff and students usually have automatic access to their academic library. This usually comprises borrowing rights as well as access rights (username and password) to online services and collections (ebooks, ejournals, databases and other search tools). You may find that physical law collections form part of the main library, or are arranged in a separate law library.

Law libraries or law collections tend to differ from other subject collections because of the large number of reference materials in bound volumes. Primary sources such as legislation and case law are published chronologically and in significant numbers. Important aids for searching and using primary sources (citators, yearbooks, digests and indexes) also form part of the law library. Getting to know the layout of the law library and where the key sources are shelved is useful knowledge and can save you a lot of time.

If you are working in the legal sector, you may find your employer has its own library. Local and national professional bodies operate libraries for members. Examples in Scotland include: the Signet Library in Edinburgh, the library of the Royal Faculty of Procurators in Glasgow, and the library of the Society of Advocates in Aberdeen. Members of the Faculty of Advocates may access the Advocates Library in Edinburgh.

ONLINE RESOURCES

By and large, modern primary sources such as case law and legislation are fully available online and increasingly, official information such as command papers and other parliamentary papers is moving fully online. However, as we have noted, the law is subject to constant change and online sources can be out of date as much as a published print document may be. Being online does not guarantee the currency of a source. There is no doubt that online databases have made legal research much easier but there is a danger that the unwary researcher assumes that all online services are the same and are of equal value.

Online services of value to legal research can include freely available websites which anyone can use, or subscription databases. Both have value and are appropriate for finding different types of information. Which you choose to use will depend entirely on the task at hand. Understanding what each can offer – what information it holds in terms of currency and authority, value-added features, supporting material to help you interpret primary sources, etc – will help you decide.

Many online services reproduce information available in print, while some services are the only source of particular types of information. Those services which reproduce printed sources often add value by offering search functions and supplementary information, or by providing information in an updated format.

There is no single online source for all legal information. You should use all relevant resources to find appropriate information.

Constant change

Online resources change regularly. URLs (web addresses) alter, the design of a website can change, database content alters, and some resources can change their name or disappear altogether. Even established databases evolve, so be prepared to adapt to changes as they happen.

Internal resources

Services provided by your university or employer offer access to internal information appropriate to your study or work.

Catalogues

Most libraries have an online catalogue or a similar online search service which provides information on the print resources you have access to as well as links to electronic journals, books and other online resources. These are almost always accessible internally (on site) and remotely (off site).

Virtual Learning Environments (VLEs)

Academic institutions use VLEs to provide course materials to students like module handbooks, reading lists and lecture notes. They are also used for interactive tutorials and to submit coursework online.

Intranets

Employers use intranets and Knowledge Management (KM) systems to store and access information relevant to their business. In a law firm these may contain "know-how" documents and well-used styles as well as links to external resources.

Websites

Websites vary widely in content and quality just as printed sources can. However, the ubiquitous search engine and its widespread use to find all sorts of information can lead to overconfidence in websites generally as valid sources of quality information. Search engines are an excellent tool to locate free sources on the internet. However, it can be more efficient to use legal information "gateways". Individual websites are too numerous to list here, but a few of general use are highlighted in this chapter.

Search engines

Search engines are probably the most common way to search for information on the web. They do not require a login and, on the face of it, are really easy to use.

Entering some terms into the search box can retrieve results from a huge variety of sources. Results are ranked by relevance according to criteria. However, what those criteria are and how they are applied is complex, not always clear and can change. Google's algorithm (Page Rank) famously changes on a regular basis. Thus, what you retrieve may not be what you intended to retrieve and may be irrelevant or unreliable. Furthermore, some information indexed in online subscription databases will not be retrieved.

Search engines are an excellent tool for locating known documents and websites and may also be useful for locating some initial information about a topic. However, you cannot rely on search engines as your only, or even main, legal research tool and you should take extra care to evaluate any sources found in this way (see Chapter 10 for tips on evaluating sources).

Gateways

A gateway is a website which acts as a directory of other websites. Experts select useful sites and classify and list these by subject. In comparison with search engines, they make it easier to find more relevant information as they have already been selected for you. Gateways can be browsed by topic but may also be searched. Among the most useful legal information gateways is the Eagle-i Internet Portal for Law (http://ials.sas.ac.uk/eaglei/project/eiproject.htm) which is a dedicated high-quality portal to legal information on the web created by the Institute of Advanced Legal Studies. Coverage includes UK, European, foreign and comparative law.

Individual Websites

Individual websites may specialise in particular types of legal information. Not all sites provide reliable sources of legal information. However, some provide access to official documents and may be the most authoritative source of that information.

BAILII (http://www.bailii.org/) The British and Irish Legal Information Institute provides access to searchable databases of case law and legislation. It is part of the "free access to law" movement (http://www.worldiii.org/worldii/declaration/).

Legislation UK (http://www.legislation.gov.uk/) is the official website for UK legislation. Coverage includes all UK Public and General Acts from 1801 (though data between 1801 and 1987 may be incomplete). From 1988 onwards, Acts as enacted and revised are included. All Acts of the Scottish Parliament from 1999 onwards are included. A full list of what is covered is listed in the "Browse Legislation" page (http://www.legislation.gov.uk/browse).

Other official sources of legal information include:

- *UK Parliament* (http://www.parliament.uk/);
- *Scottish Parliament* (http://www.scottish.parliament.uk/);
- *GOV.UK* (https://www.gov.uk/) – provides access to UK government information;
- *Scottish Government* (http://www.gov.scot/);
- *Scottish Courts Service* (http://www.scoutcourts.gov.uk);
- *Europa* (http://europa.eu/) – the gateway to official European Union sources.

Online subscription services

Academic libraries will subscribe to a number of online services to support learning and teaching. These are likely to include databases, large journal collections, ebooks and reference materials. Access in a law firm may be charged according to usage. Therefore, it is important to develop effective search techniques (see Chapter 10 for search tips and strategies). As a legal researcher, you will make most frequent use of legal databases.

You will not usually have access to every subscription service. This book covers the most frequently used services.

Access

Online subscription services require authentication to access them as the contents are protected by licence. All staff and students in academic institutions are given login credentials (username and password).

Services usually have separate log-in pages for academic and commercial users. You should access services via the log-in page recommended by your university or employer.

Full text and abstracting services

"Full-text" services allow you access to the full text of entire documents.

Indexing and abstracting services help you to locate material by providing details of where a document is published, often with an abstract (summary). You can then use the details to find the full text from other sources.

Most databases are hybrid, meaning they have a combination of full text and bibliographic records. For example, *Westlaw UK*'s "Journals" search integrates the *Legal Journals Index* and full-text journals. This allows the retrieval of article abstracts with links to the full text of articles where available. These hybrid services retrieve a wider range of material and alert you to additional documents not available in full text on the service.

If you retrieve abstracts with no link to a full-text document this does not mean that your institution does not have access to the full text. You should check for the full text from another resource (journal A–Z list or database).

Content, searching and browsing

Databases have unique content and content that is also available elsewhere. Using different databases may require you to use different search techniques. Information about content, coverage and how to search and browse effectively is usually available from links within individual database services. Although no one really likes to take the time to use help pages or guides, a quick 10 minutes to familiarise yourself with search tips will save you time in the long run.

Content   When searching a database you should be aware of what information it contains. There is no point in looking for journal articles in a database which contains only case law. Furthermore, articles from a particular journal may be available on one database service but not another.

Searching   Database services offer various options for searching by entering relevant terms. These include a general search across all databases and specialised searches for specific types of material (eg cases, legislation or journals). Searches can be basic or advanced. Basic searches can be easier to use, while advanced searches allow you to refine your search and retrieve more relevant results.

Browsing   Browsing can be a useful alternative to searching and a good way to familiarise yourself with the content in a database.

Database services

Legal databases provide access to many separate databases through a single web-interface. You can search across case law, legislation, journal articles and commentary. The precise content to which you have access is dependent on the subscription your library has. The services most widely available to Scottish law students are *Westlaw* and *Lexis®Library*.

Westlaw

Westlaw UK provides access to the full text of legislation, case law, many legal journals, and EU materials. It has the advantage of pulling together both primary (legislation, cases) and secondary (books, journals) legal information.

Westlaw's *Legal Journals Index* provides abstracts of journal articles published in the UK. Legislation and Case Analysis documents give supplementary information about cases and legislation – including their current status. Some key commentary titles are also available on *Westlaw*.

Non-UK material is available with a subscription to "*Westlaw International*".

Lexis®Library

Lexis®Library also provides access to legal information from the UK and EU. This includes the full text of legislation, case law, and a number of legal journals. Commentary varies with subscription but can include the *Stair Memorial Encyclopaedia* (see Chapter 9 for a description of the *Encylcopaedia*).

Lexis®Library's home page provides a simple search but content is also indexed in "Cases", "Legislation", "Commentary", and "Journals" pages, which can be searched individually.

Material from non-UK jurisdictions is available with a relevant subscription.

Other online database services

Other services you may have access to include:

* *Justis* – this service provides access to a range of case law, legislation, EU law, and parliamentary materials. The *JustCite* service is a legal reference search engine and citator which indexes and links to legislation, case law and articles from other subscription and public access services.

* *Lawtel* – this current awareness service includes short "Case Reports", a "Legislation Service", and an "Articles Index". Specialist subscriptions include "Human Rights" and "Personal Injury" services.

* *HeinOnline* – this service includes a (largely US) "Law Journal Library" archive as well the "English Reports", and a "Legal Classics Library" of historically important texts.

* *House of Commons Parliamentary Papers* – provides access to papers from 1688 onwards.

* *Public Information Online* – includes UK parliamentary materials from 2006/07 onwards and Scottish parliamentary materials (Session 3, 2007–).

Many other specialist legal databases exist and you may need to access non-legal databases while undertaking research. You should find out what you have access to through your library.

CURRENT LAW

The *Current Law* printed legal information service offers an alternative way to find legal information when online sources are not available.

Current Law provides information about developments in the law since 1947. Between 1948 and 1990 a separate *Scottish Current Law* service included material from the general service but with the addition of material relating solely to Scotland. From 1991 there has been a single service covering the whole of the UK. The service comprises: the *Monthly Digest*, *Year Book*, *Citators* and the *Statutes* service. The *Citators* help you to trace developments in case and statute law. *Current Law Statutes* reproduces Acts of the UK and Scottish Parliaments with annotations.

Information about *Current Law Statutes* and the *Legislation Citator* is given in Chapter 4. Information about the *Case Citator* is detailed in Chapter 7.

Monthly Digest and Year Books

Monthly Digest

The *Monthly Digest* is published monthly and provides summaries of developments in case law and legislation as well as summaries of journal articles and law books.

Digest summaries, or "items", are arranged under subject headings in separate sections according to jurisdiction (Scottish material is in a separate section). Each numbered item includes a reference to the summarised case, legislation, article etc, which you can use to find the full-text document.

The *Monthly Digest* also includes various tables after the summaries. Tables include:

- various tables of legislation (including commencement information);
- *Cumulative Table of Cases* – gives references to that year's case summaries by month and item number (eg **Jan** 372);
- progress of Bills in the UK and Scottish Parliaments; and
- Words and Phrases Judicially Considered.

A *Cumulative Index* gives references to summaries from that year's issues by month and item number. A list of *Law Publications* published during that month follows the index and a table of legal abbreviations appears at the front of each issue.

Year Book

The annual *Year Book* consolidates each year's *Monthly Digests*. Items are arranged under subject headings but are renumbered and may be re-edited.

There are now two volumes of the *Year Book* for each year:

- tables now appear at the front of volume one;
- digest summaries follow and are spread across both volumes;
- lists of words and phrases judicially considered and law books, together with the index, are found at the back of volume two.

Summaries in the *Year Book* are referred to elsewhere in the *Current Law* service by year and item number:

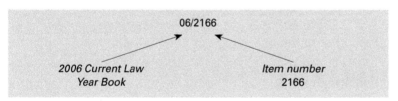

06/2166

2006 Current Law
Year Book

Item number
2166

NB If there is no two-digit year reference then the reference is to an item in the *Current Law Consolidation 1947–1951* volume.

European Current Law

In addition, *European Current Law* (1993–) provides information on European legal developments. It comprises the *European Current Law Year Book* and *Monthly Digest*.

Essential Facts

- Arrangement of legal materials varies from library to library. You should become familiar with your library's layout. Use the online catalogue to locate material in your library.
- Use library guides and web pages and attend induction tours to learn about the arrangement of materials, borrowing, and other library services.

- Online sources of legal information may be provided by your university/employer or by external organisations. External sources may be freely available or may require a subscription.
- It can be more efficient to search for good-quality websites using "gateways" rather than a general search engine.
- Subscription services require you to log in with a username and password. This is usually supplied by your university or employer.
- The most widely available subscription databases are *Westlaw* and *Lexis®Library*.
- The range and content of databases available to you depends on the subscription your library has.
- Database services can be searched or browsed. Information on how to do this is usually provided within the service.
- *Current Law* is a printed legal information service which covers developments in the law since 1947 (1948 for Scottish content). It is comprised of the *Monthly Digest*, *Year Books*, *Citators*, the *Statutes* service and *European Current Law*.

Further Reading

- F Grant, *Legal Research Skills for Scots Lawyers* (3rd edn, 2014), Chapters 1, 2 and 8.
- P Clinch, *Using a Law Library: a student's guide to legal research skills* (2nd edn, 2001), Chapters 1 and 3.
- J Knowles, *Effective Legal Research* (4th edn, 2016), Chapters 1 and 2.

3 INTRODUCTION TO LEGISLATION AND THE PARLIAMENTARY PROCESS

Legislation is the most important source of law within the Scottish legal system. It emanates ultimately from the authority of a legislature and includes Acts of Parliament (the primary legislation of the UK, also referred to as "statutes") as well as legislation passed by delegates such as the Scottish Parliament or local authorities. It also includes European Union legislation (discussed further in Chapter 8).

Historically, the pre-1707 Scottish Parliaments also created legislation. A few of these "Scots Acts" are still in force today. However, many have been either expressly repealed or have fallen into desuetude. That is to say, through lack of use or lack of modern relevance, they are no longer considered enforceable.

How to read, find and update enacted legislation is covered in Chapter 4. However, other publications which relate to the work of the UK and Scottish Parliaments are considered here. These "parliamentary publications" may be used for several purposes:

- to make you aware of likely future developments in the law;
- to study the development of the law in the past; and
- to act as an aid to statutory interpretation where *Pepper* v *Hart* criteria are met.

UK PARLIAMENTARY LEGISLATION

Primary legislation: Acts of Parliament

Parliamentary legislation is initiated mainly by the Government and tends to introduce changes to society which reflect the policies of a particular Government. Proposals for an Act of Parliament take the form of a Bill and, during the opening ceremony of Parliament, the Queen will generally outline the forthcoming Bills for the year ahead. Bills themselves fall into three distinct categories. Public Bills are the most important and take up the majority of parliamentary time since they deal with matters of important principle and generally affect society as a whole.

There are two types of Public Bill: Government Bills and Private Members' Bills. Government Bills are introduced by the ruling government of the day and generally reflect current policy or manifesto commitments. The majority of Acts passed by Parliament originate from Government Bills; Private Members' Bills, on the other hand, generally originate from an individual MP. These Bills will more often than not deal with an area which does not receive Government backing or is controversial and they often reflect personally held beliefs of MPs. In some cases, controversial measures for which a Government does not want to take responsibility may be introduced by back-benchers, with the Government secretly or openly backing the measure and ensuring its passage. Such Bills are sometimes known as "Government handout Bills"; the Abortion Act 1967 was passed in such a manner. This type of Bill ensures that back-benchers have more input into the legislative process of Parliament, but the success of such Bills is very limited. Most Private Members' Bills fail to become an Act.

The second category of Bills is known as Private Bills. These contain proposals which generally affect the interests of specified persons or localities. They are introduced through petition by the persons or organisations who desire the Bill. Private Bills are commonly introduced by local authorities or public corporations and seek to give statutory powers to those bodies which they would otherwise not have. For example, at time of writing, the City of London Corporation (Open Spaces) Bill seeks to make provision relating to the public open spaces under the management and control of the City of London Corporation. Private Bills follow a slightly different procedure in their enactment from other Bills and there is often very little discussion of such Bills within Parliament.

The third and final category of Bills is called Hybrid Bills. These are normally Government Bills which specifically affect particular individuals or groups. They are therefore treated in many ways like Private Bills. An example of such a Bill can be found in the Channel Tunnel Bill of 1986, now the Channel Tunnel Act 1987. The Bill was generally public in nature, given that it set out to create the Channel Tunnel; however, certain sections of the Act gave the Government powers of compulsory purchase to buy areas of land in Kent required to build the tunnel. Since these sections specifically affected only Kent landowners, the Bill was hybrid in nature. More recently, the High Speed Rail (London–West Midlands) Bill has similarly been confirmed as being hybrid in nature.

Subordinate legislation

It is common for Parliament, through an Act, to confer on Ministers or other executive bodies the power to make rules and regulations which have the force of law and are thus properly called legislation. The phrase "subordinate legislation" covers every exercise of such power and is sometimes also known as "delegated legislation". The power to enact this kind of legislation comes from an authorising or "parent" Act which will be an Act of Parliament. There are many types of subordinate legislation but the most common are Statutory Instruments and Orders in Council. More than 3,000 of these are passed every year and they have a number of advantages and uses:

- Parliament has time to concern itself only with the broad principles of Acts. Detailed regulations and rules should be dealt with by the administration. The Road Traffic Acts are a good example. The Road Traffic Act 1972 empowered the Secretary of State to make regulations for the use of vehicles on public roads; such detail cannot possibly be set out in an Act of Parliament. Thus subordinate legislation can save parliamentary time.

- Subordinate legislation allows the knowledge and experience available outside Parliament to be utilised through appropriate consultation. For example, in issuing regulations under the Dangerous Dogs Act 1991, the Secretary of State must consult with the British Veterinary Association.

- In times of emergency, it is impossible to pass an Act of Parliament quickly enough to deal with the situation. Subordinate legislation can be passed rapidly and allows responsiveness to emergencies. For example, the Secretary of State for the Environment, Food and Rural Affairs could restrict the movement of livestock if there was an outbreak of Foot and Mouth Disease.

- Subordinate legislation is also used to give effect to Acts of Parliament. Often an Act of Parliament will state that all, or some, of the Act is to come into force on a date to be set by the Secretary of State. This is done using a Statutory Instrument known as a "commencement order".

Statutory instruments

Statutory instruments (or SIs) are also known as "Regulations" or "Rules" and the power to make them will be delegated to a Minister by an Act of Parliament. Most statutory instruments are "laid" before Parliament.

However, they are not scrutinised to any great extent. If the authorising Act states that an instrument is to be passed using the *negative* procedure, then it will come into force in 40 days unless either House of Parliament resolves that it should be annulled. This is a fairly weak form of control.

The second method of laying an SI before Parliament involves the *affirmative* procedure. Under this method, the SI requires parliamentary approval before it can come into force. This is achieved through a 90-minute debate in Parliament. If a resolution to pass the SI is not achieved then it will be taken back and amended in order for re-submission. This is obviously a slightly stronger form of control than the negative procedure.

Many statutory instruments have no laying requirement at all. This is not uncommon and regularly applies to commencement orders.

Orders in Council

Orders in Council refer to the Privy Council which advises the Queen on matters of constitutional importance. There are two types of Order in Council: those made under the authority of the Royal Prerogative, and those which are delegated to Ministers through an Act of Parliament. The first is an Order which is made without requiring the consent of Parliament. Such Orders are usually reserved for matters of constitutional importance. They are made by the Privy Council with the authority of the Queen; although the Queen's assent today is purely formal and in reality is exercised by Ministers on her behalf. The second type of Order is authorised by an Act of Parliament and cannot be made without parliamentary approval. Such an Order was used to transfer powers from the UK Ministers to the Scottish Parliament under the devolution settlement.

Orders in Council do not really differ in status from that of statutory instruments but are considered through custom and convention to be more dignified and are therefore used for matters of constitutional importance.

Control of subordinate legislation

Challenge in the courts is not possible for Acts of Parliament, but it is for subordinate legislation. This is because the legislative powers of the UK Parliament are unlimited, whereas those of Ministers and subordinate bodies are not. There are two main grounds of challenge in the courts:

- that the content or substance of the legislation is *ultra vires* the parent Act (in other words, it goes beyond the powers authorised by the Act); and

- that correct procedures have not been followed in the making of the legislation.

Parliamentary stages of Bills

Bills may be introduced in either the House of Commons or the House of Lords. However, there are a number of Bills which must always originate in the Commons, such as Money Bills and Bills of constitutional importance. A Bill which originates in the House of Lords will progress through the same stages as those in the House of Commons. The stages of a Bill as it passes through Parliament are as follows:

- **First Reading** The first stage consists of a number of formalities where the Bill is announced and its short title is read out. A date is set for the Second Reading of the Bill and from here the Bill will be printed and distributed.

- **Second Reading** At this stage, the House will debate the general principles contained in the Bill. At the end of the debate, the motion is put to a vote. It is very rare for a Government Bill to lose a vote, although it is not unheard of. For example, the Shops Bill 1986 was lost at the Second Reading.

- **Committee Stage** During the Committee Stage, most Bills are passed over to a Public Bill Committee which is created for the specific purpose of dealing with the Bill. Public Bill Committees generally consist of between 16 and 20 MPs and reflect the state of the parties represented in the House of Commons. At this stage, the Bill is subjected to what is supposed to be a thorough line-by-line examination and any of its clauses may be amended where necessary. However, most Government Bills have a Programme Motion which sets out the timetable or "guillotine" for the Bill after the Second Reading. As a result of the guillotine some clauses may receive no scrutiny by the Committee. Evidence may be taken from experts and interest groups. A small number of Bills at this stage are passed over to a Committee of the Whole House as opposed to a Public Bill Committee. During such a Committee, each clause of the Bill is debated on the floor of the House of Commons by all MPs. Such a Committee is used for Bills of constitutional importance, such as the Scotland Bill during 1998. It is also used to pass Bills which require a rapid enactment, such as the annual Finance Bill.

- **Report Stage** If a Bill has come from a Committee of the Whole House, then this stage is purely a formality. However, for the majority of Bills, this stage will involve a review of any amendments made during the Committee Stage. All members of the House have an opportunity to debate at this stage, making it rather more democratic than the Committee Stage where the scope for debate is rather limited. There is no vote at this point.

- **Third Reading**   Here, the House examines the final version of the Bill. The Bill is debated in principle and a vote taken. This stage is usually very brief since no major amendments may be made.

A key problem with the legislative process of the Commons is the amount of time it takes. The more amendments a Bill receives, the longer it will take to pass through Parliament. Consequently, many Bills are subject to what is called a "guillotine" motion. Such a motion will quickly bring the debate on a Bill to an end, allowing it to proceed more quickly. Since 1999, the Commons has also used a new procedure known as the "programme" motion. Using this motion, a programme or timetable is put before the House, agreeing the amount of time allocated to stages of a Bill and dates for progression.

- **Lords Stages**   Once the Commons stages have been completed, the Bill is sent to the House of Lords, where the whole procedure is repeated. The Lords stages are similar in many ways to those of the Commons, except for a few key differences. The Committee Stage in the Lords always consists of a Committee of the Whole House and there is no use of "guillotine" or "programme" motions which allow for unrestricted debate on the principles of a Bill. It is also possible to table amendments during the Third Reading in the Lords.

  Changes made to a Bill in the House of Lords result in an extra stage in the Commons known as the Considerations of Lords Amendments. This is necessary in order to approve any amendments made by the Lords. Occasionally, the two Houses will not agree on a Bill. In such circumstances, the House of Lords can exercise its delaying power and refuse to accept the proposals of the House of Commons. However, this delaying power is limited by the Parliament Act 1911, as amended by the Parliament Act 1949, which states that the Lords can delay a Bill only for up to one year. Using the Parliament Acts, the House of Commons can then submit a Bill for Royal Assent without the consent of the House of Lords. Examples of Acts passed in this way include the War Crimes Act 1991 and the Hunting Act 2004. Thus, the power of the House of Lords to block legislation permanently is curtailed. Unless the House of Commons invokes the Parliament Acts, then both Houses of Parliament must always agree in order for the final Bill to progress.

- **Royal Assent**   This is the final stage of a Bill, where the Crown must formally assent to the Bill in order for it to become an Act of Parliament and pass into law. In modern times this has become something of a formality since the UK is a constitutional monarchy and the sovereign is bound to assent to any Bill, except in extraordinary circumstances. The last time assent was given by the Crown in person was in 1854 and assent has not been refused since 1707 when Queen Anne refused to consent to the Scottish Militia Bill.

UK PARLIAMENTARY PUBLICATIONS

Types of UK parliamentary publication

Bills

A Bill is first published "as introduced" to either House and is given a unique Bill number accordingly. For example, the Data Retention and Investigatory Powers Bill introduced to the House of Commons in session 2014–15 was allocated number 73 (shown on the Bill document as HC Bill 73 in round brackets after the Bill title). When the Bill was introduced in the House of Lords it was given the number 37. As amendments are made, they may be published as separate documents, or the Bill may be republished to incorporate amendments. (**NB** When a Bill is republished it receives a new Bill number.) Government Bills are now accompanied by Explanatory Notes, which outline what the Bill is designed to achieve. The UK Parliament website has a comprehensive guide to the passage of a Bill at http://www.parliament.uk/about/how/laws/passage-bill/.

Command Papers

Command Papers are Governments papers presented to Parliament, nominally "by command" of the Queen (in practice often by a Government Minister or other body). They represent decisions and information that the Government wants to refer to one or both Houses of Parliament. They include "White" and "Green" papers (regarding government policy and proposed legislation), state papers (treaties), reports of Royal Commissions, some reports of the Law Commission of England and Wales, and some pre-devolution reports of the Scottish Law Commission. They are published as a series.

House of Commons (HC) and House of Lords (HL) Papers

HC and HL Papers represent the work of both Houses including the formal authoritative record of decisions, reports from Select Committees, daily and weekly reports of written answers and questions, register of Members' interests and other reports.

Hansard (Official Report of Parliamentary Debates)

Hansard (also known as Parliamentary Debates or the Official Report) contains edited reports of debates and other parliamentary business in both Houses. It comprises *House of Commons Debates*, *House of Lords Debates* and *Public Bill Committee Debates* (formerly *Standing Committee Debates*). Verbatim debates are recorded daily, edited and made available online on the UK Parliament website. The final versions are subsequently made available as hard copy bound volumes.

Where to find UK parliamentary publications

Websites

UK Parliament website (http://www.parliament.uk/) provides comprehensive access to Parliamentary publications, many of which are now only available in electronic format.

Under "Parliamentary Business", you can access:

- "Bills before Parliament" and an archive of previous sessions (from 2001 onwards including all Bill documents and links to debates at all Bill stages);
- "Committee Publications" from the late 1990s onwards;
- House of Commons and House of Lords business papers; and
- *Hansard* including HC Debates (1988–), HL Debates (1995–) and Public Bill/General Committee/Standing Committee Debates (1997/98–). *Historical Hansard* covers the period *1803–2005.*

GOV.UK publications website (http://www.gov.uk/government/publications/) hosts Command Papers originating in Government departments from May 2005 onwards.

Print sources

Sessional Papers   Printed copies of Public Bills, Command Papers and HC and HL Papers are held by many university and large research libraries. These may be bound into "Sessional Papers" for each House.

Older bound Sessional Papers are often arranged by broad subject and bound in separate volumes (as organised by the Stationery Office). From 1979/80 onwards, the different categories of paper are commonly bound in separate numerical sequences according to type of material (eg Command Papers, HC Papers, Public Bills). A "Sessional Index" to papers is usually contained at the end of a session's volumes.

Hansard The printed version of *Hansard* is also held by many university and large reserach libraries. It may be catalogued as *Hansard*, Parliamentary Debates or Official Report.

Online subscription services

Public Information Online is a web-based archive of searchable Parliamentary Papers and Official Documents. The contents of this service and current content include the following (but note that an ongoing digitisation project means that access to older material will continue to extend back in time):

- HC Papers (2006–), HC Bills (2006–), HL Papers (1955–), HL Bills (1956–), and Command Papers (1963–);
- Standing and Public Bill Committees (2006–);
- HC and HL *Hansard* (2008/09–).

House of Commons Parliamentary Papers (HCPP) This service covers the period from 1688 onwards and provides access to House of Commons Sessional Papers (ie Public Bills, HC Papers and Command Papers) as well as *Hansard* from 1803 onwards.

How to find UK parliamentary publications

Aids to finding UK parliamentary publications

Online services (including those described above) enable browsing or searching for publications, usually by title, date or subject. The online subscription service, *UKOP* is the official catalogue of UK official publications. It provides bibliographic information for publications from the UK and Scottish Parliaments as well as other public bodies from 1980 onwards. It is updated daily.

Lawtel UK, a subscription service, provides information about Bills and Command Papers.

Printed indexes for *Hansard* and the Sessional Papers are produced for each session.

Citation

Forms of citation to parliamentary materials vary, but examples include:

Hansard

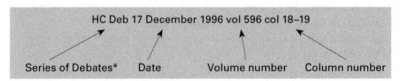

* House of Commons (HC) or House of Lords (HL)

Public Bill Committee Debates

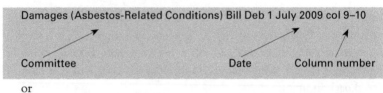

or

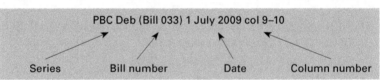

Standing Committee Debates may be cited as:

> SC Deb (A) 30 Jan 2003 col 217
> or Stg Co Deb (2002–2003) Co A Local Government Bill col 217

House of Commons Papers

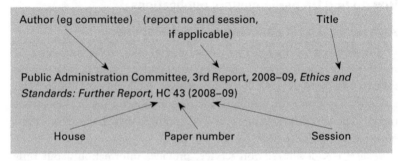

NB HC Papers may be cited simply by HCP number and session:

> HC 43 (2008–09)   or   HC (2008–09) 43

House of Lords Papers

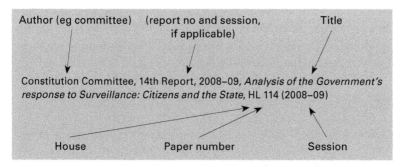

NB HL Papers may be cited simply by number and session:

HL 114 (2008–09)   or   HL (2008–09) 114

Public Bills

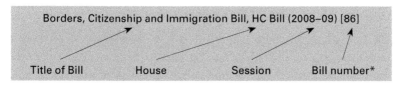

Command Papers

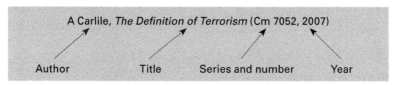

NB The abbreviation of "command" is important in identifying the relevant series of papers:

–	1–4222	1st series	1833–1869
C	C 1–C 9550	2nd series	1870–1899
Cd	Cd 1–Cd 9239	3rd series	1900–1918
Cmd	Cmd 1–Cmd 9889	4th series	1919–1956
Cmnd	Cmnd 1–Cmnd 9927	5th series	1956–1986
Cm	Cm 1–	6th series	1986–

Finding Sessional Papers

Print Sources Use catalogues or printed indexes (eg Sessional Indexes) to search for the Paper or Bill by subject or title. Sessional Indexes list the

Paper or Bill number. Bound volumes of Sessional Papers from 1979/80 onwards are commonly arranged by parliamentary session and then in separate numerical sequences according to type of material (eg Command Paper, HC Paper, HC Bill). Use the parliamentary session and number to find the paper in the numerical sequence.

For older bound Sessional Papers you may need to use the session's index to discover the paper's page number within the bound volumes.

Online Use search and browse functions on the UK Parliament website, *TSO Official Documents*, *Public Information Online* or *HCPP* to search by publication title or number, subject, author, date, etc

UKOP allows you to search using a variety of criteria. Links to the full text of some documents are available, but you may need to follow up references elsewhere.

Tracing the progress of UK Bills

WEBSITES

UK Parliament website The "Bills before Parliament" page (http://services.parliament.uk/bills/) lists Bills from the current and previous sessions with links to information about their state of passage, debates, explanatory notes and all amendments.

Print sources The progress of current Bills can be checked using the *House of Commons Weekly Information Bulletin* or *Current Law Monthly Digest* "Progress of Bills" table.

ONLINE SUBSCRIPTION SERVICES

Public Information Online The "Bill Tracker" allows you to trace the progress of a Bill through Parliament.

- Bills are listed by Parliament and session, then alphabetically.
- Follow the link to the Bill you wish to track.
- Documents associated with the Bill are listed with links to the full text.

Lawtel The *Lawtel UK* "Parliamentary Bills" search allows you to follow the progress of Bills. The Bill record lists the different stages and links are provided to available documents on the UK Parliament website.

Finding debates on a Bill

WEBSITES

UK Parliament website   From the *Hansard* pages http://www.parliament.uk/business/publications/ you can find a debate by:

- *Reference*: browse by series (eg HL/HC), date/volume, and column number.
- *Subject*: follow the link to the relevant index (entries link to the relevant section in *Hansard*).
- *Speaker*: follow the relevant "View by Member" link, and then browse by Member, then date or subject.

Alternatively, link to the *Hansard* debates from the Bill page on the UK Parliament website http://services.parliament.uk/bills/.

Print sources   To find a debate by subject (eg Bill) or a speaker you can use:

- *Current Law Statutes*: annotations at the beginning of an Act provide references to debates on the related Bill.
- Explanatory Notes: recent UK Acts' Explanatory Notes contain references to debates on the related Bill under "Hansard References".
- Indexes to *Hansard*: look up the subject or speaker. The indexes give references to volume and column number.

Use the *Hansard* reference information to locate the debate by the series (HC, HL, PBC), volume, and column number.

ONLINE SUBSCRIPTION SERVICES

Public Information Online   Use this service to find a debate by:

- *Reference*: follow the link to "UK Parliament" then to "HOL/HOC Daily Hansards" or "Public Bill and General Committee Debates". Then browse by session, volume/committee, and date.
- *Subject/Speaker*: follow the link to the "Search" screen. Under "Categories" select "HOL/HOC Daily Hansards" and enter terms in the "Keywords in document text" field.

Westlaw UK   The "Annotated Statutes" service provides "*Pepper* v *Hart* notes", which provide references to relevant debates in *Hansard*.

Annotations, if available, appear within individual provision records below the text of the Act.

SCOTTISH PARLIAMENTARY LEGISLATION

On 1 July 1999, the Queen officially opened the Scottish Parliament. The Scotland Act 1998 created the Scottish Parliament by devolving various powers from the UK Parliament and handing them over to the Scottish Parliament. Of those devolved powers, arguably the most important is the power to make law. The Scotland Act states that the "... Parliament may make laws, to be known as the Acts of the Scottish Parliament" but the power to make such laws is not unlimited.

The Scottish Parliament is a creature of statute and can only pass laws in areas where it has legislative competency. This is because the UK Parliament has not passed all of its law-making powers to the Scottish Parliament. The Scotland Act 1998 does not state which powers have categorically been given to the Scottish Parliament since the Scotland Act subscribes to the retaining model of devolution. Under this model, everything is devolved to the Scottish Parliament except a number of specific areas which are "retained". These retained areas are listed within the Scotland Act and dictate the legislative competence of the Scottish Parliament.

The legislative competence of the Scottish Parliament is clearly spelled out in s 29 of the Scotland Act:

- the Scottish Parliament may not legislate for another territory;
- the Scottish Parliament may not legislate on a matter reserved to the UK Parliament by virtue of Sch 5;
- the Scottish Parliament may not legislate in breach of the restrictions contained in Sch 4;
- Acts of the Scottish Parliament must be compatible with the Human Rights Act 1998 and the European Communities Act 1972; and
- the Scottish Parliament may not remove the office of Lord Advocate.

In terms of Sch 5 to the Scotland Act, there are a number of areas which are known as "reserved" areas and here the Scottish Parliament has no power. The reserved areas are split into both "general" and "specific" reservations. General reservations deal with subjects such as defence, social security and foreign affairs. These are areas where the law generally needs to be uniform across the UK or must be retained in order to fulfil international obligations. Specific reservations are very detailed and provide particular named areas where the Scottish Parliament has no power. The list is long and includes such areas as abortion; space exploration; interference with time zones; and xeno-transplantation.

The law-making powers of the Scottish Parliament were further increased by the Scotland Act 2012 which devolved a variety of additional powers. These powers include:

- the administration of elections to the Scottish Parliament;
- the regulation of airguns;
- responsibility for aspects of licensing and control of controlled substances;
- regulation of drink-driving limits;
- the determination of the national speed limits in Scotland;
- the power to vary income tax for Scottish taxpayers by up to 10 per cent;
- greater borrowing powers; and
- control of various minor taxes including a new land and buildings tax and control over business rates and a Scottish Landfill tax.

The Smith Commission and the Scotland Bill 2015

During September 2014, a cross-party commission was established under the Chairmanship of Lord Smith of Kelvin to examine and make recommendations for the devolution of further powers to the Scottish Parliament. In November 2014 the Commission published its recommendations, which included *inter alia* the following recommendations:

- The Scottish Parliament to have complete power to set income tax rates and bands.
- The Scottish Parliament to receive a proportion of the VAT raised in Scotland, amounting to the first ten percentage points of the standard rate.
- UK legislation to state that the Scottish Parliament and Scottish Government are permanent institutions. The Parliament will also be given powers to legislate over how it is elected and run.
- The Scottish Parliament to have power to extend the vote to 16- and 17-year-olds, allowing them to vote in the Scottish General Election in 2016.
- The Scottish Parliament to have control over a number of welfare benefits.

- Responsibility for the management of the Crown Estate's economic assets in Scotland, including the Crown Estate's seabed and mineral and fishing rights, and the revenue generated from these assets, to be transferred to the Scottish Parliament.
- The Scottish and UK governments to draw up and agree on a memorandum of understanding to ensure that devolution is not detrimental to UK-wide critical national infrastructure in relation to matters such as defence and security, oil and gas and energy.

At time of writing (February 2016) a Scotland Bill is making its passage through Parliament. Almost all of the recommendations of the Smith Commission mentioned above are incorporated in the clauses of the Bill.

Bills and parliamentary stages

Like Acts of the UK Parliament, Acts of the Scottish Parliament must begin as Bills. A Bill may be introduced by a member of the Scottish Executive (now known as the "Scottish Government"), a Committee of the Scottish Parliament, or an individual MSP. Prior to the introduction of a Bill, a member of the Scottish Executive must make a statement that the provisions of the Bill are within the legislative competence of the Parliament. The Presiding Officer must also consider the provisions and make a similar statement to the Parliament as to whether or not the Bill is competent.

There are four main categories of Bill which can be brought before the Scottish Parliament. These are Executive Bills, Committee Bills, Members' Bills and Private Bills. As a general rule, there is extensive consultation and pre-legislative scrutiny on a Bill before it is introduced to the Parliament. All Bills on introduction must be accompanied by a Financial Memorandum setting out estimates of the administrative and compliance costs of the Bill. Furthermore, all Executive Bills must be accompanied by Explanatory Notes summarising the provisions of the Bill, and a Policy Memorandum which sets out the policy objectives of the Bill. The parliamentary process that a Bill follows will vary depending on the type of Bill but the most common procedure is that used for Executive Bills which consist of three stages:

- **Stage 1: Report** The Bill is referred to the relevant subject committee, known as the "lead committee", for consideration of its general principles. The lead committee can take evidence at this stage and other committees with an interest in the Bill may also be involved in putting forward their views, for example the Finance Committee. The lead committee prepares a report which is submitted to the Parliament where a debate and vote are held on the principles of the Bill.

- **Stage 2: Committee** Detailed scrutiny of the Bill by the lead committee takes place. The Bill is considered section by section and amendments are considered. Each section must be agreed by the lead committee. If the Bill is amended, at least 10 sitting days must elapse before the Bill proceeds to Stage 3 (4 days if there are no amendments).

- **Stage 3: Plenary** The Bill returns to the Parliament for further consideration. The Parliament must decide whether the Bill in its final form should be passed and at least a quarter of all MSPs must vote.

Following the final vote in the Parliament there must be a 4-week period before the Bill is submitted for Royal Assent. This time gap allows certain Law Officers, namely the Advocate General, the Lord Advocate and the Attorney-General, to have a role in the scrutiny of Bills. During this period, if any of the Law Officers doubts whether any provision is within the legislative competence of the Scottish Parliament, then they may refer the issue to the Supreme Court. This power may be similarly exercised by a Minister of the UK Parliament. If the Supreme Court finds that the Bill is outwith the legislative competence of the Parliament, then the Bill must be returned to the Parliament in order for amendments to be made. If the amended Bill is then subject to no further challenge, the Presiding Officer submits it to the Queen for Royal Assent.

Committee Bills

Committee Bills are seen as an innovation of the Scottish Parliament and a modern addition to the law-making process. The White Paper *Scotland's Parliament* suggested that legislation should be initiated by committees of the Scottish Parliament, in keeping with the spirit of giving more MSPs a greater role in the legislative process of the Parliament. Committee Bills allow a committee of the Parliament to conduct inquiries into an area of law where it is perceived that change is required. The committee may then submit a report on this to the Parliament. With the agreement of the Parliament, the Scottish Executive then has 5 days to decide whether or not to support the report and propose legislation. If the Executive does not itself agree to bring forward legislation in line with the committee's proposals, then the Parliament may decide to adopt the Bill and bring forth draft legislation. The draft Bill would then be introduced to the Parliament and be subject to a general debate on its principles. If approved in principle, then the Bill would generally follow the same procedure outlined for an Executive Bill. The first Committee Bill was introduced by the Justice 1 Committee in 2001 and was enacted as the Protection from Abuse (Scotland) Act 2001.

Members' Bills

These are similar to Private Members' Bills within the UK Parliament. Individual MSPs are entitled to bring forward proposals for legislation before either the Parliament or a relevant committee. If an MSP submits proposals to a committee, then the committee may hold an inquiry in order to assess whether the legislation is required. If the committee decides to proceed with the proposals then the Committee Bill procedure will be used. Alternatively, if an MSP submits proposals to the Parliament, then they must have the support of at least 18 other MSPs. After lodging the Bill with the Parliamentary Clerk, if the Bill receives 18 signatures within 1 month, then it will proceed following the Executive Bill procedure. One of the most high-profile Members' Bills was the Protection of Wild Mammals (Scotland) Bill introduced by Lord Watson which subsequently received Royal Assent in 2002.

Private Bills

Private Bills may be introduced by a person, body or association in order to gain powers in a specific area. They may be introduced to the Parliament on any sitting day. Private Bills generally follow the Executive Bill procedure; however, during Stage 1, the committee may require additional information and may ask the proposer to advertise the Bill in order to allow for any objections. The Committee must then prepare a report which deals with the need for such legislation and incorporates any public objections. The first Private Bill introduced in the Parliament was the Robin Rigg Offshore Wind Farm (Navigation and Fishing) (Scotland) Bill which received Royal Assent in 2003.

Subordinate legislation of the Scottish Parliament

The Scotland Act 1998 conveys powers to make subordinate legislation upon Scottish Ministers, Ministers of the Crown and Her Majesty in Council. This is necessary for the same reasons that the UK Parliament requires power to enact Statutory Instruments and Orders in Council. Statutory instruments of the Scottish Parliament are known as Scottish statutory instruments or SSIs. Although Scottish Ministers normally make subordinate legislation only in areas where the Parliament has legislative competence, provisions exist which also allow them to legislate in areas where the Parliament has no competence. The Scotland Act 1998 allows a UK Minister to transfer functions, by Order in Council, to Scottish Ministers and these functions may then be exercised in so far as they relate to Scotland. There are some restrictions placed upon the power to make subordinate legislation. Such legislation cannot create serious criminal offences, and it is also subject to the same principles of challenge as UK subordinate legislation, for example the *ultra vires* doctrine.

Of particular note are Acts of Sederunt and Acts of Adjournal. Acts of Sederunt are rules created by the Court of Session, which govern procedure in civil courts. Acts of Adjournal are rules created by the High Court of Justiciary, which govern procedure in criminal courts. Despite their name, these are *not* Acts of Parliament. In recent years they have been published as SIs and, since devolution, as SSIs.

SCOTTISH PARLIAMENTARY PUBLICATIONS

Types of Scottish parliamentary publication

Publications relating to the work of the Scottish Parliament include:

Bills (SP Bills)

A Bill is first published "as introduced" to the Parliament and is given a Bill number. At each stage, the Bill is republished to incorporate amendments but retains its original number. Executive Bills are accompanied by "Explanatory Notes" which explain what the Bill seeks to achieve, a "Financial Memorandum" which explains what it is likely to cost, and a "Policy Memorandum" which explains policy objectives and gives details of previous consultation.

Scottish Parliament Papers (SP Papers)

These include reports of Committees and other publications resulting from the work of the Parliament.

Scottish Parliament Official Report

This provides a record of debates on Bills and other business before the Parliament. Constituent parts include: Meetings of the Parliament, Committee Meetings, and Written Answers.

Scottish Government Papers (SG Papers)

Formerly published as "Scottish Executive Papers" (SE Papers), these include publications from the Scottish Government and reports and accounts of devolved agencies and other public bodies. Post-devolution Scottish Law Commission Reports may be published as SG/SE Papers.

Where to find Scottish parliamentary publications

Websites

Scottish Parliament (http://www.scottish.parliament.uk/home.htm) The official website provides access to publications including:

- the Official Report: follow links to "Parliamentary Business" then to "Official Report";
- SP Bills: follow links to "Parliamentary Business" then to "Bills"; and
- Committee reports etc (issued as SP Papers): follow links to "Parliamentary Business" then to "Committees".

Scottish Government (http://www.scotland.gov.uk/Home) The "Publications" link provides access to Government and agency publications including some SG Papers.

Print sources

Printed copies of SP Bills, SG/SE Papers, SP Papers, and the SP Official Report are collected by some university libraries.

Online subscription services

Public Information Online Scottish parliamentary content includes:

- SP Papers, SP Bills, and the Official Report from Session 3 (2007–) onwards
- SG Papers (2008–).

How to find Scottish parliamentary publications

Aids to finding Scottish parliamentary publications

Search and browse functions on subscription databases and websites help you search by publication title, number, subject or date. *UKOP* provides bibliographic information about some Scottish Parliament and Scottish Government publications. *Lawtel UK* provides information about SP Bills.

Bibliographies of Scottish Parliament Publications and lists of "Laid Papers" (eg SG Papers) are provided on the Research briefings and factsheets page at http://www.scottish.parliament.uk/parliamentary-business.aspx/. There are links to the Current Series and Historic Series.

Citation

Official Report

Meeting of Parliament:

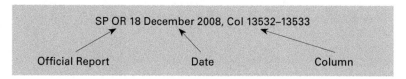

Committee Meetings:

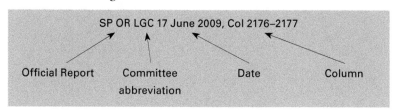

Written Answers:

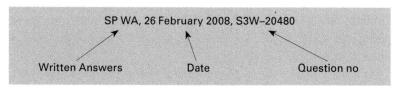

Bills

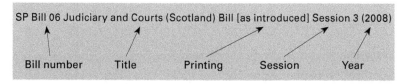

SP Bills keep their number on reprinting; revisions are indicated after the Bill number:

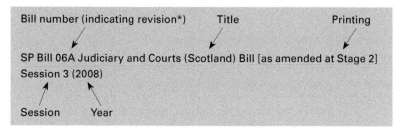

SP Papers

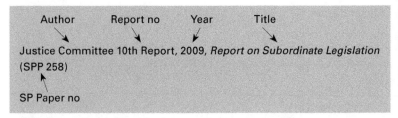

SG Papers (SE papers)

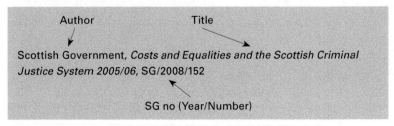

Finding SP Papers, SP Bills, and SG Papers

Online Use search and browse functions on the *Scottish Parliament* website or *Public Information Online* to search by publication title or number, subject, author, date, etc

If using *UKOP*, you can search using a variety of criteria. However, while links to the full text of some documents are available, you may need to follow up references elsewhere online or in print.

Tracing the progress of SP Bills

WEBSITES

Scottish Parliament website The "Bills" page (http://www.scottish. parliament.uk/parliamentarybills.aspx) provides links to "Current Bills" and "Previous Bills". Each Bill's page lists the stages the Bill has reached with links to all associated documents including explanatory notes, research briefings, amendments and debates.

ONLINE SUBSCRIPTION SERVICES

Public Information Online The "Bill Tracker" allows you to follow the progress of a Bill through the Scottish Parliament.

- Bills are listed by Parliament and session, then alphabetically.
- Follow the link to the Bill you wish to track.

- Documents associated with the passage of the Bill are listed with links to the full text.

Lawtel   A *Lawtel UK* "Parliamentary Bills" search allows you to follow the progress of Bills in the Scottish Parliament.

- The Bill record lists the different stages with dates.
- For Bills currently in progress, links are provided to available documents on parliamentary websites.

Finding debates on an SP Bill

WEBSITES

Scottish Parliament website   The "Parliamentary Business" page (http://www.scottish.parliament.uk/business/index.htm) provides separate "Official Report" and "Motions Questions and Answers" links.

To access the Official Report, follow the link "Official Report" where you can find a debate by SP OR reference:

- *Meetings of Parliament*: use "Chamber Official Reports" to locate "Meeting of the Parliament" by date.
- *Committee Meetings*: choose "Committee Official Reports" to find Committee Meetings by session and date.

To find a debate by subject (eg Bill):

- Follow the link "Alphabetical List of Debates" from the Official Report page and browse by session then debate.

Alternatively, access the Bill page on the Scottish Parliament website (http://www.scottish.parliament.uk/parliamentarybusiness/bills.aspx/) to link to debates in the Official Report from the Bill page.

To access Written Answers, follow the link "Motions, Questions and Answers" then the link "Written Answer Reports" or "Previous Written Answer Reports" to find Written Answers by date.

Alternatively, choose "Motions, Questions and Answers search" to search by:

- *Keyword*: enter search terms.
- *MSP*: use the drop-down menu to choose the MSP or Law Officer field.
- *Date range*: select from the drop-down options or enter a range of dates.

Print sources   To find a debate by subject (eg Bill) or a speaker you can use:

- *Current Law Statutes*: annotations at the beginning of an Act contain references to debates relating to the Bill.
- "Explanatory Notes" to Acts of the Scottish Parliament contain references to debates on the related Bill (under "Parliamentary History").

Use the SP Official Report (OR) or Written Answers (WA) reference to locate the debate by series/committee, session, and column.

ONLINE SUBSCRIPTION SERVICES

Public Information Online   The service can be used to locate debates in the Official Report by:

- *Reference*: follow the link to "Scottish Parliament" then to "Official reports", "Written Answers", or "Official Reports of Committee Debates". Then browse by session and date ("Committee Debates" can be browsed by committee – select "Alphabetical by Title" from the "Sort" drop-down menu).
- *Subject/Speaker*: follow the link to the "Search" screen. Under "Categories" select "Scottish Parliament Official Reports". Enter terms in the "Keywords in document text" search field.

Westlaw   The "Annotated Statutes" service provides *"Pepper* v *Hart* notes", which provide references to relevant debates in the Official Report.

BYELAWS

As well as subordinate legislation emanating from both the UK and Scottish Parliaments, there exists another form of subordinate legislation which is known as a byelaw. Byelaws are rules made by an authority subordinate to Parliament for the regulation, administration or management of a certain district and/or property. In Scotland, byelaws are made by local authorities and certain other public bodies such as railway authorities. However, the vast majority of byelaws are enacted by local authorities by virtue of the Local Government (Scotland) Act 1973. The 1973 Act states that local authorities may make byelaws for the good rule and government of their area. A common example is the "anti-drinking" byelaw adopted by Scottish local authorities which bans the consumption of alcohol within certain public areas. Such byelaws must satisfy a number of conditions. They must be within the authority of the authorising statute and must not be contrary to the general law of the land. In addition, they must be certain in their enactment and not unreasonable. Byelaws are capable of being challenged in court as *ultra vires* if they fail to adhere to these conditions and have not been made by following the prescribed procedure.

Byelaws have the same effect as any other law, provided that they are validly enacted. Before being deemed valid, a byelaw must be confirmed by a relevant Scottish Minister. Prior to confirmation, the local authority must inform members of the public of its intention to legislate. This is done by printing a notice in the local newspaper and informing the public where copies of the draft byelaw can be obtained. This procedure allows citizens to lodge any relevant objections. Such objections must be taken into account by the Scottish Ministers who then have the power to confirm, modify or refuse the byelaw. Once a byelaw has been confirmed, it must be publicised in the area concerned. Local authorities are also obliged to keep a register of byelaws for their area in order to allow public inspection.

Essential Facts

UK Parliament

- An Act of Parliament usually requires the consent of the House of Commons and the House of Lords, and the Assent of the Monarch.
- Acts of Parliament may be passed without the consent of the House of Lords, utilising the Parliament Acts of 1911 and 1949.
- There are two types of Public Bills: Government Bills introduced by the ruling government of the day and Private Members' Bills introduced by individual MPs.
- Private Bills contain proposals which generally affect the interests of specified persons or localities. They are introduced through petition by the persons or organisations who desire the Bill.
- Hybrid Bills are normally Government Bills which specifically affect particular individuals or groups.

Scottish Parliament

- An Act of the Scottish Parliament requires the consent of the Scottish Parliament and the Assent of the Monarch.
- The Scottish Parliament is a creature of statute and can only pass laws in areas where it has legislative competency.
- There are four main categories of Bill which can be brought before the Scottish Parliament. These are Executive Bills, Committee Bills, Members' Bills and Private Bills.
- Executive Bills are introduced by the ruling government of the day.
- Committee Bills allow a committee of the Scottish Parliament to conduct inquiries into an area of law where it is perceived that change is required. With the agreement of the Scottish Parliament, legislation may then be proposed.
- Members' Bills are introduced by individual MSPs.
- Private Bills may be introduced by a person, body or association in order to gain powers in a specific area.

Parliamentary publications

- UK parliamentary publications include: Bills, House of Commons and House of Lords Papers, Command Papers, and *Hansard*.
- Scottish parliamentary publications include: SP Bills, SP Papers, and the Official Report. SG Papers are also relevant to the work of the Parliament.
- UK and Scottish parliamentary publications are available in print and from online public access and subscription services. The Parliaments' websites are useful sources for these publications.

Further Reading

- J McFadden and D McFadzean, *Public Law* (3rd edn, 2016), Chapters 6 and 8.
- F Grant, *Legal Research Skills for Scots Lawyers* (3rd edn, 2014), Chapters 5–7.
- J Knowles, *Effective Legal Research* (4th edn, 2016), Chapter 6.
- P Clinch, *Using a Law Library: a student's guide to legal research skills* (2nd edn, 2001), Chapters 4, 8, 10 and 13.

- J W Colquhoun, *Finding the Law: A Handbook for Scots Lawyers* (1999), Chapter 7.
- G Holborn, *Butterworths Legal Research Guide* (2nd edn, 2001), Chapters 4 and 7.

4 FINDING AND USING UK AND SCOTTISH LEGISLATION

In order to find and use legislation effectively, it is important to understand both how legislation is structured and how legislative provisions can change over time.

Once legislation is enacted it does not necessarily come into force automatically. Furthermore, the version of legislation originally published does not necessarily remain the version in force in perpetuity. Legislation may require subsequent legislation to bring it into force and may be amended by later legislation. Indeed, once provisions are repealed or revoked, they cease to be in force. Not all provisions of UK legislation extend to Scotland. Conversely, the territorial extent of some provisions is restricted to Scotland.

In addition, the meaning of legislation is subject to judicial consideration in case law. This process of "statutory interpretation" is discussed in detail in Chapter 5.

Here, we focus on the structure of Acts of the UK and Scottish Parliaments and on how to find UK and Scottish legislation. We also look at how to check whether legislation has come into force, been amended or repealed, whether provisions extend to Scotland, and whether legislation has been subject to judicial consideration.

UK AND SCOTTISH ACTS: CATEGORISATION, AMENDMENT AND STRUCTURE

Categorisation of Acts

Acts, like Bills, may be categorised according to the scope of their effect.

UK Acts are categorised as:

- *Public General Acts*: these are now the most common type of Act passed. Unless otherwise stated, a Public General Act is presumed to apply to the whole of the UK. However, the territorial extent may be limited to a particular area, eg Scotland or England and Wales.
- *Local Acts*: these only affect a particular restricted area of the country.
- *Personal Acts:* these only affect a particular individual or body (eg a company).

Acts of the Scottish Parliament (asps) are similarly categorised as being public and general in application or as being private Acts, which have local or personal effect. However, the scope of an asp does not affect the way it is cited in the same way as it affects a UK statute.

In general terms, the purpose of an Act is to bring about a change in the law. However, there are some types of Act which serve a particular purpose. Examples include:

- *Constitutional Acts* have great constitutional significance, eg the European Communities Act 1972 incorporates EU law into UK law. The Scotland Act 1998 enabled Scottish devolution and, together with the Human Rights Act 1998, imported the European Convention on Human Rights into Scots law.
- *Codifying Acts* aim to set out a particular area of law in a single statute and may incorporate existing statute and common law sources.
- *Consolidating Acts* similarly aim to simplify an area of law by placing the provisions of several existing Acts into a single new Act.
- *Statute Law Revision Acts* are designed to repeal existing legislation which has become obsolete.
- *Amendment Acts* aim specifically to amend, or update, previous legislation.

Amendments and repeals

Whatever purpose an Act is designed to achieve, it will often change the law by amending or repealing the provisions of existing legislation. This may be done by sections of a new Act identifying words which are to be removed in an earlier Act and supplying words which are to be substituted or added into the text of the earlier Act. A later Act may repeal entire sections from, or insert entire sections into, an earlier Act. If created under appropriate powers, delegated legislation may also amend or repeal an Act.

For example, the original version of s 1(2) of the Divorce (Scotland) Act 1976 provided:

"(2) The irretrievable breakdown of a marriage shall, subject to the following provisions of this Act, be taken to be established in an action for divorce if—

(a) since the date of the marriage the defender has committed adultery; or

(b) since the date of the marriage the defender has at any time behaved (whether or not as a result of mental abnormality and whether such behaviour has been active or passive) in such a way that the pursuer cannot reasonably be expected to cohabit with the defender; or

(c) the defender has wilfully and without reasonable cause deserted the pursuer; and during a continuous period of two years immediately succeeding the defender's desertion—

    (i)   there has been no cohabitation between the parties, and

    (ii) the pursuer has not refused a genuine and reasonable offer by the defender to adhere; or

(d) there has been no cohabitation between the parties at any time during a continuous period of two years after the date of the marriage and immediately preceding the bringing of the action and the defender consents to the granting of decree of divorce; or

(e) there has been no cohabitation between the parties at any time during a continuous period of five years after the date of the marriage and immediately preceding the bringing of the action."

But this original text has been amended by ss 11 and 12 of the Family Law (Scotland) Act 2006:

"11 Divorce: reduction in separation periods

In subsection (2) of section 1 of the 1976 Act (irretrievable breakdown of marriage to be sole ground of divorce)—

(a) in paragraph (d), for 'two years' there shall be substituted 'one year'; and

(b) in paragraph (e), for 'five' there shall be substituted 'two'.

12 Irretrievable breakdown of marriage: desertion no longer to be ground

Paragraph (c) of section 1(2) of the 1976 Act (irretrievable breakdown of marriage to be sole ground of divorce) shall be repealed."

So the amended s 1(2) of the Divorce (Scotland) Act 1976 reads as follows (amended or repealed text is indicated by square brackets):

"(2) The irretrievable breakdown of a marriage shall, subject to the following provisions of this Act, be taken to be established in an action for divorce if—

(a) since the date of the marriage the defender has committed adultery; or

(b) since the date of the marriage the defender has at any time behaved (whether or not as a result of mental abnormality and whether such behaviour has been active or passive) in such a way that the pursuer cannot reasonably be expected to cohabit with the defender; or

[...]

(d) there has been no cohabitation between the parties at any time during a continuous period of [one year] after the date of the marriage and immediately preceding the bringing of the action and the defender consents to the granting of decree of divorce; or

(e) there has been no cohabitation between the parties at any time during a continuous period of [two] years after the date of the marriage and immediately preceding the bringing of the action."

Structure of an Act

Modern UK Public General Acts and Acts of the Scottish Parliament usually comprise the following elements:

- *Contents* – outline the structure of the Act.
- *Short title* – an Act is usually referred to by short title. Older Acts did not have short titles but many have had these assigned retrospectively.
- *Year and chapter (or asp)* – modern UK statutes are assigned a chapter number according to the order in which they gained Royal Assent in a calendar year: chapter 1 is the first Act passed in that year, chapter 2 the second, and so on.

    Acts of the Scottish Parliament are assigned an "asp" number rather than a chapter number.
- *Long title* – this is more detailed than the short title and indicates the Act's purpose.
- *Date of Royal Assent* – in UK Acts this date, in square brackets after the long title, is when the Bill was passed by Parliament and became an Act. This is not necessarily the date all, or any, of the Act comes into force.

    Acts of the Scottish Parliament include a note of the date the Act was passed by the Parliament *and* the date the Act received Royal Assent; this precedes the long title.
- *Standard enacting formula* – Acts include this to indicate they have parliamentary authority.
- *Sections* – Acts are divided into numbered "sections". Sections may be divided into numbered subsections (subsection numbers appear in

rounded brackets). Sections and subsections may be further divided into paragraphs (indicated by a lower case letter in rounded brackets) and subparagraphs (indicated by a lower case Roman numeral).

Longer Acts may be divided into large numbered "parts" and then into "chapters". However, sections continue to be numbered consecutively throughout the whole Act.

- *Interpretation section* – this may be found towards the end of some Acts and indicates the meaning to be given to certain words used in the Act.
- *Commencement section* – this may be found towards the end of the Act and contains details of when sections of the Act are to come into force. If the Act has no commencement provisions then it is presumed to come into force at the beginning of the day it receives Royal Assent.
- *Short title section* – restates the short title by which the Act may be cited.
- *Geographic extent section* – in UK Acts this section indicates which sections of the Act apply to which parts of the UK. If a UK Act contains no information about extent, it is presumed to apply to the whole UK.

   NB Provisions regarding interpretation, commencement, short title and extent may often be combined in a single section.

- *Schedules* – often appear at the end of an Act and provide the detail of provisions laid out in the preceding sections of the Act. There is often a schedule listing legislation affected by the Act such as those previous Acts which are amended or repealed. Schedules are divided into paragraphs and subparagraphs.
- *Marginal notes* – do not form part of the Act but are printed beside the main text. They offer a brief description of sections' content and aid navigation round the Act.

Explanatory Notes do not form part of the Act and are published separately. These are now officially produced for UK Public General Acts and Acts of Scottish Parliament which were introduced as government Bills (except Budget Bills). These may be used in the interpretation process.

WHERE TO FIND UK AND SCOTTISH LEGISLATION

Original and revised forms of legislation

A piece of legislation may be amended by other subsequent legislation. When using legislation, you need to be aware of whether the source you use provides legislation in its original form or in a revised version.

- Original, or unrevised, versions do not take account of amendments by subsequent legislation.
- Revised, or consolidated, versions aim to incorporate subsequent amendments and present legislation in an up to date form.

In either case, you should check whether subsequent amendments have been made since the version you are using was created.

Online subscription services

Westlaw   *Westlaw* contains English/UK Public General Acts which were still in force in 1991 and those passed subsequently, as well as public Acts of the Scottish Parliament. *Westlaw* contains a "selection of UK SIs of general application published between 1948 and 1991" and all subsequent SIs and SSIs. There is also a selection of Westminister Parliamentary Bills from 2015–2016 onwards.

Legislation retrieved through a basic search represents the revised version and incorporates amendments. Historic versions of some legislation are available.

The *Westlaw Annotated Statutes* service provides expert analysis which aims to help interpretation and application of legislation. The service covers legislation from 2007 onwards and analysis of earlier legislation will be added on an ongoing basis. Annotations are indicated in search results and full-text documents. The "annotation window" is displayed below the text of the provision.

Lexis®Library   *Lexis®Library* contains revised versions of in force Public General Acts and SIs which apply to England and Wales. Some provisions of pre-devolution UK Acts and SIs which relate only to Scotland are not included.

Revised versions of in force public Acts of the Scottish Parliament and SSIs are included.

Lawtel   *Lawtel* includes the unrevised version of UK Public General Acts (1987–) and Acts of the Scottish Parliament (1999–). *Lawtel* indexes SIs/SSIs (1987–) with links to the unrevised full text where available.

Justis   *Justis* contains unrevised legislation including English/UK Public General Acts (1235–), Acts of the Scottish Parliament (1999–), SIs, and SSIs.

Websites

Legislation.gov.uk (http://www.legislation.gov.uk/) is the official website for UK legislation and carries most types of legislation and their explanatory notes. Coverage includes:

- UK Public and General Acts 1801–1987 (incomplete); 1988–present;
- UK Statutory Instruments 1948–1986 (incomplete); 1987–present;
- Acts of the Scottish Parliament 1999–present; and
- Scottish Statutory Instruments 1999–present.

The "Browse Legislation" page (http://www.legislation.gov.uk/browse) has a full list of all types of legislation held in the database and their coverage (shown by year).

BAILII (http://www.bailii.org/) The *British and Irish Legal Information Institute* website (*BAILII*) provides access to both unrevised and revised versions of UK Acts as held on the Legislation UK website.

Records of the Parliaments of Scotland to 1707 (RPS) (http://www.rps. ac.uk/) This site contains comprehensive coverage of the proceedings of the Scottish Parliaments from 1235 to 1707. This includes unrevised Scots Acts. The version available on *RPS* may differ from the authoritative version. It is of primary significance as a historical record rather than a database of legislation though there are useful tables of statues by reign.

Print sources

Authoritative print series of legislation include:

Public General Acts and Measures These contain the official versions of UK Acts and do not include amendments or annotations. The official version is referred to as the "Queen's Printer" copy. It is this version which should be cited in court (though taking account of amendments). Modern bound volumes are arranged by year and chapter number.

Older Acts of the Parliaments of England and Great Britain are available in *Statutes of the Realm* (1235–1713, also available on *HeinOnline*) and various editions of *Statutes at Large* (also available on *Eighteenth Century Collections Online*).

Acts of the Scottish Parliament The "Queen's Printer" copies of the devolved Scottish Parliament's Acts contain no amendments and no annotations. Acts are arranged by year and asp number.

Acts of the Parliaments of Scotland 1124–1707 (the "Record edition") This 19th-century publication, edited by T Thomson and C Inness, has been considered to be the authoritative version of pre-1707 Scots Acts.

The Acts of the Parliaments of Scotland 1424–1707 (HMSO, 2nd edn, 1966) This small volume contains the text of those pre-1707 Scots Acts still in force when it was published in 1966 and has a useful index to pre-1707 Acts.

Statutory Instruments Official copies of statutory instruments contain no amendments and no annotations. Bound volumes are now arranged by year and SI number.

Scottish Statutory Instruments These again contain no amendments and no annotations. The arrangement is by year and SSI number.

Independently published print series reproducing legislation include:

Current Law Statutes This series comprises annual "bound volumes" and the "Service File". Between 1949 and 1990 there was a separate *Scottish Current Law Statutes Annotated* service.

The bound volumes reproduce the original text of:

- UK Public General Acts from 1948 onwards (1949 onwards for Scottish material);
- UK Private Acts from 1992 onwards; and
- Acts of the Scottish Parliament.

Legislation remains unrevised. However, *Current Law Statutes* is particularly useful because it incorporates annotations, which are not part of the Acts' original text. Annotations, written by a subject expert, explain the impact of, and give background to, the text of the Act. Annotations include references to debates on a Bill, reported in *Hansard*. The text of the Act is in larger type while annotations are in smaller type.

The arrangement of Acts in the annual bound volumes is: UK Public General Acts, UK Private Acts, then Acts of the Scottish Parliament. Acts are then arranged by chapter or asp number.

Bound volumes now include the following information for each year:

- Alphabetical and Chronological Tables of Statutes;
- UK and Scottish Commencement Diaries;
- A Table of Parliamentary Debates; and
- UK and Scottish Indexes.

The *Service File* binders contain the current year's Acts. The "Current Awareness" binder contains commencement information as well as statute and SI citators for the current year.

Scots Statutes Revised (in 10 volumes) contains public Acts from the period 1707–1900, applicable to Scotland, which remained unrepealed at date of publication. There is a separate volume of Scots Acts (1424–1707).

Scots Statutes contains statutes applicable to Scotland produced during the period 1901–1948.

Other series of statutes include *Halsbury's Statutes of England and Wales*, the *Law Reports Statutes*, *Public General Acts affecting Scotland* (*Blackwood's Acts*) and *Statutes Revised*.

Textbooks and encyclopaedias Revised versions of legislation are available in a range of textbooks and encyclopaedias.

Student statute collections concerning a particular area of law collect together relevant UK and Scottish Acts, SIs, SSIs, together with EU legislation and other relevant materials. Examples include *Blackstone's Statutes on Company Law* or *Avizandum Legislation on the Scots Law of Obligations*.

"Looseleaf" encyclopaedias for specific areas of law provide relevant revised legislation. As amendments are made, old pages are removed and new updated pages inserted. Scottish examples include *The Scottish Planning Encyclopedia* and *Parliament House Book*.

HOW TO FIND AND CHECK THE STATUS OF LEGISLATION

Citations to legislation

UK Acts

Short title UK Acts may be cited by "short title". For example:

> **Children (Scotland) Act 1995**

Year and chapter Alternatively, UK Acts may be cited by year and chapter. Since 1963 the year cited is the calendar year (eg 1995) and the chapter number is assigned in the order in which Acts gain Royal Assent in a given year.

Public General Acts are cited in the form:

> 1995 Chapter 36
>
> or 1995 c. 36

Local Acts' chapter numbers are written in Roman numerals. For example, the Bell's Bridge Order Confirmation Act 1995 may be cited as:

> 1995 c. iv

Personal Acts' chapter numbers are written in italics. For example, the George Donald Evans and Deborah Jane Evans (Marriage Enabling) Act 1987 may be cited as:

> 1987 c. 2

Prior to 1963 Acts were cited by regnal year (year of the monarch's reign). For example, the National Galleries of Scotland Act 1906 may be cited as:

> 6 Edw. 7, c. 50

That is, the fiftieth Act to be passed in sixth year of the reign of Edward VII. **(NB** The citation of older Acts is slightly complicated by other factors. For a detailed explanation of this see P Clinch, *Using a Law Library: a Student's Guide to Legal Research Skills* (2nd edn, 2001), pp 47–49.)

Acts of the Scottish Parliament

Acts of the Scottish Parliament may be cited by short title, or by year and asp:

> Gaelic Language (Scotland) Act 2005
>
> or   2005 asp 7

Pre-1707 Scots Acts

Scots Acts may be cited by short title:

> Lawburrows Act 1429

or year and chapter:

1429 c. 20

or by reference in the "record edition":

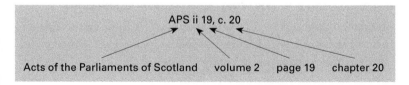

(**NB** Citation to Scots Acts is complicated by other factors: see D French, *How to Cite Legal Authorities* (1996), pp 73–74.)

Sections and Schedules

"Section" may be abbreviated to "s" so references to a section may be cited in the form: s 5 meaning "section 5".

Citations are given in the form:

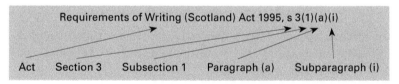

"Schedule" may be abbreviated to "Sch" and "paragraph" to "para". Therefore, paragraph 4 of Schedule 1 to the Requirements of Writing (Scotland) Act 1995 may be cited as:

Requirements of Writing (Scotland) Act 1995, Sch 1, para 4

Statutory instruments and Scottish statutory instruments

Statutory instruments may be cited by title or by year and number. For example:

The Bingo Duty Regulations 2003 or SI 2003/2503

Scottish statutory instruments may be similarly cited:

Horse Passports (Scotland) Regulations 2005 or SSI 2005/223

(**NB** In a given year SIs and SSIs are numbered in separate sequences. It is important to know to which type the year and number relates: SSI 2005/223, above, is quite different to SI 2005/223 – The Copyright (Educational Establishments) Order 2005.)

Aids to finding and checking the status of legislation

Subscription databases incorporate features which allow you to find and check the status of UK and Scottish legislation (see below). However, it is sometimes necessary to use "traditional" aids.

Current Law Legislation Citator You can use the *Legislation Citator* to track legislation's development over the period covered by the citator (1948–). For example, you can learn of any amendments or repeals to an Act or find out whether cases have interpreted sections of an Act.

The Current Law Legislation Citators (beginning in 1947) are published either in volumes spanning a few years or in single annual volumes.

NB The current year's citator is contained in the *Current Law Statutes: Service File*.

The 1948–72 volume is titled *Scottish Current Law Statute Citator* and the 1972–88 volume, *Scottish Current Law Legislation Citator*. From the 1989–95 volume onwards, the citator comprises the "Statute Citator" and the "Statutory Instrument Citator".

The "Statute Citator" lists:

- (pre-1707) Acts of the Parliaments of Scotland;
- (post-1999) Acts of the Scottish Parliament;
- Acts of the Northern Ireland Assembly; and
- UK Public General Acts.

Statutes listed are those which, during the period covered by the volume, have been passed, judicially considered, repealed, amended, or those under which subordinate legislation has been issued. Statutes are listed by jurisdiction then chronologically by year and chapter/asp. Information about pre-1707 and post-1999 Acts of the Scottish Parliament is given at the start of the "Statute Citator" (before UK Acts).

Under each individual provision (eg section) details provided include:

- amendments and repeals, with details of the amending/repealing provisions;
- names and citations of cases judicially considering the section; and
- statutory instruments issued under the section.

Information is given about legislation created both prior to, and during, the period each volume covers – but only if developments have occurred during that period (eg the 2000–2001 volume contains information about the Curators Act 1585 but only because this was repealed in 2000).

From 1993 onwards the "Statutory Instrument Citator" gives similar information relating to statutory instruments and Scottish statutory instruments. SIs are listed by year and number. Information about SSIs is given at the start of the "Statutory Instrument Citator" (before UK SIs).

Current Law Statutes: Service File   The "Current Awareness" binder contains information about legislation for the current year, including:

- a table of "Legislation Not Yet In Force";
- the current year's Statute and SI Citators (updated monthly);
- Commencement Orders and a "Commencement Diary";
- Alphabetical and Chronological Tables of Statutes; and
- a Table of Parliamentary Debates (1950–).

Chronological Table of the Statutes   These volumes list Public Acts from 1235 onwards by year and chapter/asp and give information about whether an Act has been amended or repealed. Pre–1707 Scots Acts and Acts of the Scottish Parliament are listed in separate sections. At time of writing, the latest edition (published February 2016) is up to date to the end of 2014.

Is it in Force?   The current volume contains information about the status of Acts passed since 1 January 1960. It gives details of which provisions have come into in force and by what authority. Acts are listed by year and then alphabetically by short title. An online version is available on *Lexis®Library* as "Halsbury's Is it in Force?".

Finding an Act

Traditional methods

To locate an Act in the official series *Public General Acts and Measures* or *Acts of the Scottish Parliament*, in *Current Law Statutes*, or in other print series, you must know the year and chapter/asp number.

Short Title   To find the year and chapter/asp number, you can look up the Act by "short title" in, for example:

- the alphabetical table of statutes in the *Current Law Statutes Service File*;
- the alphabetical list in recent volumes of the *Current Law Legislation Citator*.

If you know the year, you can look up the alphabetical list/index in that year's *Public General Acts* or *Current Law Statutes*.

Subject   The most efficient way to find legislation by subject is often by using a textbook or encyclopaedia in the relevant subject area. Key legislation will be referred to in the text. Textbooks and encyclopaedias often include a table of legislation cited, which usually includes year and chapter details. Use the table of statutes or index to look up legislation by title. Entries should also refer you to the page on which you can find details of the legislation.

Year and chapter/asp   Once you know the year and chapter/asp, go to the relevant year's volumes in the appropriate statute series and look up the Act by chapter/asp (chapter 1 is first in sequence, chapter 2 second, and so on).

Online

Westlaw   Follow the "Legislation" link at the top of the homepage to go to the Legislation search screen.

- *Title*: to search for an Act or SI by title enter the title in the "Act/SI Title" field. you may search for SIs by year and number (eg 2003/2503).
- *Subject*: to search for terms occurring within legislation, enter these in the "Free Text" field.
- *Provision*: you may specify a provision by selecting provision type from the drop-down menu and entering the number in the "Provision Number" field.

"Search Results" for a search by title display the title of legislation with a link to the "Arrangement of Act" (or SI). The "Arrangement of Act" screen lists individual provisions with links. (**NB** Results for a search including a free text term or provision number may display direct links to individual provisions.)

After following a link to a provision, the right frame displays the provision and in the left frame is a link to "Legislation Analysis", which provides lots of additional information such as cases citing the provision or journal articles or books discussing it. Legislation retrieved is the revised version.

Tip: To view an entire Act, follow the link (shown as a PDF document icon) labelled "PDF of entire Act" at the top of the "Arrangement of Act" screen, or from within individual provision records.

Lexis®Library From the home page choose "Legislation" from the toolbar to go to the Legislation search screen. You can search by:

- *Title.*
- *Year and chapter (etc)*: enter the year in the "Year" field and the chapter, asp, SI number in the "Series number" field.
- *Subject*: to search for terms occurring within legislation, enter these in the "Search terms" field.
- *Provision*: enter the appropriate number in the "Provision" field.

In the results list, click the title link to view full text. Use the arrows to move between sections or click on the PDF link (if available) to view the entire piece of legislation.

UK Legislation website (http://www.legislation.uk/) You can search or browse for legislation. To browse, choose the type of legislation (eg UK Public General Acts) and simply choose the relevant year. (Years are shown on a bar graph with the number of Acts passed in that year.) Acts are listed in chapter order (ie the order in which they received Royal Assent) with the most recent at the top.

You can search by "short title", "chapter number", "provision" and "type of legislation" as appropriate.

The Act is displayed with all sections and schedules, which you can select to read in full. There are also PDF files of the Act as originally enacted and as revised. If there are any pending amendments not yet included in the record, this will be stated on the screen beside the Act.

Lawtel The "Statutes" search allows you to enter terms in "Title and Year of Publication" and "Free Text" fields or select "Subjects" from a list.

Justis/JustCite The "Legislation" search screen on *Justis* allows you to enter terms in "Title", "Full Text", and "Reference" (eg year and chapter) fields.

JustCite's "Legislation" search allows you to search by title and "reference". Search results link to documents which give information about the Act and provide links to available full-text sources.

Checking the status of an Act

When using legislation you must be aware of:

- whether a particular provision has come into force;

- whether the provision is still in force or has been repealed (in the case of an SI "revoked"); and
- whether a provision has been amended by subsequent legislation.

If you are using a reliable revised version then you need only check for amendments from the date to which the version is up to date.

You may also need to know whether a provision extends to Scotland and whether it has been judicially considered or interpreted in a case.

Checking whether a section of an Act has come into force

Traditional methods

Commencement section The first place to look is the "commencement section" within the Act itself. This section may specify that particular sections of the Act are to come into force:

- on the day it received Royal Assent;
- at a specified date thereafter; or
- at a date to be appointed by, for example, a government minister.

If the Act has no commencement provisions, then it is presumed to come into force at the beginning of the day it receives Royal Assent.

If the commencement section indicates that powers have been delegated to a minister to bring the Act into force, you need to check whether a "Commencement Order" (a type of SI) has been issued for relevant sections.

Is it in Force? If the Act was passed since 1960, refer to *Is it in Force?* The entry for each Act indicates which section contains commencement provisions, lists the relevant Commencement Orders, and the date (if any) at which it came into force.

Current Law Statutes Refer to the *Table of Legislation Not Yet in Force* in the *Current Law Statutes Service File*. If the section of the Act is not listed, this may indicate that it has come into force. The "Commencement Diary" in the "Commencement Orders" section of the "Current Awareness" binder gives the commencement date of provisions recently brought into force.

Current Law Legislation Citator Alternatively, refer to the relevant volumes of *Current Law Legislation Citator*. Start with the volume covering the date of the Act and trace forward. The entry for each Act lists Commencement Orders issued during the period covered by each volume. Refer to the relevant Order to check the date at which a section came into force.

Daily List   For very recent commencement information, check the *Daily List* (http://www.tso.co.uk/daily_list/issues.htm). This list of TSO publications is produced daily. It includes a "Commencement Orders" section, which lists Orders issued on a particular date with details of provisions brought into force together with the commencement date.

Online

Westlaw   You can check for commencement information for an individual provision or the entire Act:

- *Individual Provision*. From the provision record follow the link to the "Legislation Analysis" document. Under "Commencement" the date the section came into force is noted with details of relevant commencement provisions. If the provision is not in force this will be noted as "Date not available (not yet in force)".
- *Entire Act*. Commencement information for the entire Act can be viewed by following the link to the "Overview Document".

NB *Westlaw* does not give complete commencement information for legislation prior to 1991.

Lexis®Library   Search for the Act using the Legislation search screen (choose "Legislation" from the toolbar). On the right of the screen for the entire Act and for all sections, the "Find out more" box gives a link to the online version of (Halsbury's) *Is It In Force?* Click on this to see the commencement information for all sections of the Act (or for the particular provision you are looking at).

Lawtel   Each record of an Act retrieved from a "Statutes" search in *Lawtel UK* provides a link to a "Statutory Status Table". This table provides commencement information section by section. Information is available from 1984 onwards.

UK Legislation   Refer to the Commencement section of the Act (usually at the end of the Sections, before the Schedules). Links are provided (where appropriate) to delegated legislation bringing the Act into force.

Justis/JustCite   From a *Justis* legislation document, information about Commencement Orders related to a section is available under the *JustCite* "Amended by" tab for the section. This information is also available in documents retrieved through a *JustCite* "Legislation" search.

Checking whether an Act or section has been repealed or amended

Traditional methods

Current Law Legislation Citator   Start with the volume covering the date of the Act and trace forward in time, volume by volume. In each volume, find the Act by year and chapter/asp number:

- The entry for each Act lists, section by section, amending/repealing legislation issued during the period covered by each volume.
- You must look at the amending legislation to check exactly when, and how, the original legislation was amended.

NB The *Legislation Citator* only covers the period from 1948 onwards. For amendments and repeals prior to that date, refer to the *Chronological Table of Statutes*.

Chronological Table of the Statutes   Look up the Act by year and chapter/asp:

- An Act repealed in its entirety is listed with its title in *italics* and the repealing legislation is referred to.
- An Act which remains at least partially in force is listed with its title in **bold**. Any repealed or amended provisions are noted together with the amending legislation.

Online

Westlaw   The basic "Legislation" search retrieves revised legislation, so incorporates repeals and amendments. Amendment and repeal information is available from:

- *Individual provision.* Within the provision record, text inserted or repealed by amending legislation is indicated by the text appearing within square brackets and repealed text is indicated by a series of dots in square brackets [...]. Footnotes indicate the repealing/amending legislation. The "Table of Amendments" allows you to view previous versions of the provision.

- *Entire Act.* Amendment and repeal information for an entire Act is listed in the "Overview Document".

NB Detailed information is only available for amendments/repeals made in the period since information was uploaded to Westlaw (in 1991). Nevertheless, amendments prior to that date are incorporated.

Lexis®Library   Check for repeals or amendments using:

- *Legislation search.* This retrieves in force legislation incorporating repeals and amendments. These are indicated by text appearing in square brackets. Details of amending legislation are given, where possible, under "Notes" within the provision record. The "Find out more" box has links to *Halsbury's Statutes Citator* and *Halsbury's SIs Citator*, which provide a list of all amendments and repeals.

NB At time of writing, information for pre-devolution UK legislation affecting only Scotland is not comprehensive. *Halsbury's Citators* do not cover legislation from the Scottish Parliament.

Lawtel   Each record of an Act retrieved through a *Lawtel UK* "Statutes" search provides a link to a "Statutory Status Table". This table provides section by section, amendment and repeal information. Links to details of relevant amending or repealing legislation are given under the "Notes" heading. Information is available from 1984 onwards.

UK Legislation   (http://www.legislation.gov) The "List of all changes" to the Act are given in the "More Resources" page. Note, however, that all amendments prior to 2002 are already incorporated in the legislation on this database so only details of changes made since 2002 are listed.

Justis   From a *Justis* legislation document, amendments information is available under the *JustCite* "Amended by" tab. This information is also available in documents retrieved through a *JustCite* "Legislation" search. Follow links to amending legislation in order to update the text of the Act.

Checking whether a provision extends to Scotland

Traditional methods

This information is contained within the Act itself in the "extent section", which gives information about the territorial extent of provisions. If a UK Act contains no information about territorial extent, it is presumed to apply to the whole UK.

Online

Westlaw   From an individual provision record, follow the "Legislation Analysis" link. Under the "Extent" heading, the territorial extent of the provision is noted.

UK Legislation   (http://www.legislation.gov.uk) Extent information is provided near the end of the Act. Geographical extent is a searchable feature of legislation on the "Advanced Search" screen.

Checking whether a provision has been judicially considered

Traditional methods

Current Law Legislation Citator   Begin with the volume covering the date the Act was passed and trace forward in time, volume by volume. In each volume, find the Act by year and chapter/asp. The entry for each Act lists, by section, notable cases reported during the period covered by each volume.

Online

Westlaw   Information about cases citing a legislative provision can be found from "Legislation" and "Cases" searches.

- *"Legislation" search*. From an individual provision record follow the "Legislation Analysis" link. Under the "Cases Citing" heading is a list of cases citing the legislation.
- *"Cases" search*. Follow the link to "Advanced Search". Enter the short title of the Act in the "Legislation Title" field, and the section number in the "Legislation Provision No." field. The results list contains records of cases citing the provision.

Justis/JustCite   In a *Justis* legislation document, the *JustCite* "Subsequent Cases" tab provides information about judicial consideration. This information is also available in documents retrieved through a *JustCite* "Legislation" search.

Essential Facts

- UK and Scottish legislation can be found from a variety of official and subscription print and online sources.
- When using legislation you need to know whether it has come into force, been amended or repealed, extends to Scotland, or has been judicially interpreted. You can use functions on online databases or use the *Current Law Legislation Citator* to check this. Open access websites are of limited value for this.
- The most useful version of legislation is often a revised version, which incorporates amendments (revised legislation is available on *Westlaw*, *Lexis®Library*, the *UK Legislation* website and in various textbooks and encyclopaedias).

Further Reading

- R M White, I D Willock and H L McQueen, *The Scottish Legal System* (5th edn, 2013), Chapters 7 and 8.
- F Grant, *Legal Research Skills for Scots Lawyers* (3rd edn, 2014), Chapters 5–7.

5 INTRODUCTION TO STATUTORY INTERPRETATION

Often the language used in a statute will be ambiguous or unclear. This is when statutory interpretation becomes an important legal mechanism for ascertaining what the precise intention of the legislature was when the statute was written. Statutory interpretation involves the courts attempting to look behind the plain and ordinary meaning of words within a statute in order to glean what the precise legislative intent may be. There are a number of traditional approaches to statutory interpretation which are used in the UK, and are outlined as follows.

TRADITIONAL APPROACHES TO STATUTORY INTERPRETATION

Originally, there were three different approaches to interpreting statutes. These became known colloquially as the three rules of statutory interpretation, namely the literal rule, the golden rule and the mischief rule.

The literal rule

The literal rule involves the courts applying the ordinary, natural or dictionary meaning of words within the statute:

> "If the words of the statute are in themselves precise and unambiguous, then no more can be necessary than to expound those words in their natural and ordinary sense. The words themselves alone do, in such case, best declare the intention of the law giver." (*Sussex Peerage Claim* (1884))

Thus in applying this rule, if a clear meaning appears, then the courts must apply that meaning and not question whether that meaning actually and sensibly represents the intention of the legislature. Use of the literal rule can result in absurdities and as such it is highly criticised by many lawyers. For example in the case of *Whitely* v *Chappell* (1869), the defendant had fraudulently voted in the name of a deceased person. Legislation stated that it was an offence to impersonate any person entitled to vote. However, in applying the literal rule, it was held that a dead person was not entitled to vote, and thus the defendant had committed no offence. The literal approach was very common in 19th-century Britain due to the preoccupation with formalism at that time. It is a less popular approach in modern times and is often cited as producing inequitable results.

The golden rule

The golden rule is inextricably linked to, and flows from, the literal approach. If the meaning of words, when interpreted using the literal rule, gives rise to an absurdity in the law, then the courts are entitled to assume that the legislature did not intend such an absurdity. In turn, the courts may then construe the words in such a way to give meaning to the actual intention of Parliament. Thus the golden rule is generally used to correct absurdities. For example in *Holliday* v *Henry* (1974) it would have been absurd to decide that a car balanced on four roller skates was not "on" a public road for the purposes of the Vehicles (Excise) Act 1971, s 8(1).

The mischief rule

The mischief rule is the oldest of the three traditional rules and was established in *Haydon's Case* (1584). In utilising the Mischief Rule, the courts may take into account the reasons as to why the particular statute was passed, ie what was the actual "mischief" with which the legislature was trying to deal in passing the statute? For example, in *Smith* v *Hughes* (1960), the Street Offences Act 1959 made it an offence for a prostitute to solicit men in a "street or public place". The question arose as to whether a woman who drew a man's attention from her balcony by tapping and hissing was guilty of an offence under the Act. The court held that the mischief which Parliament clearly intended to legislate for was to prevent people from being pestered or molested by common prostitutes whilst walking in public streets. Therefore, the mischief would extend to prostitutes not only physically on the streets but also in areas such as doorways and balconies. The mischief rule can be effective in cases such as *Hughes*, where the mischief is clearly identifiable; however, it is not always easy to ascertain what particular mischief Parliament intends to legislate for. For example, in *Black Clawson International Ltd* v *Papierwerke Waldhof-Aschaffenburg AG* (1975), Lord Diplock noted that:

> "The mischief rule was set out at a time when statutes contained long preambles reciting the particular defect in the common law that the Act was intended to remedy. Therefore, in discovering the mischief, the courts had to look no further than the four corners of the Act. .... In construing modern statutes which contain no preamble to serve as aids to the construction of enacting words, the 'mischief' rule must be used with caution to justify any reference to extraneous documents for this purpose."

MODERN APPROACHES TO STATUTORY INTERPRETATION

The purposive approach

In recent times, the courts have taken a more purposive approach to statutory interpretation which can best be described as a continuum across the three traditional rules with particular emphasis upon the mischief rule. In utilising the purposive approach, a court must ascertain the objectives of the legislation, examine the terms of the specific section which is being interpreted, and discover what part in the general object of the legislation the particular section was intended to achieve. A court should also look beyond the four corners of the statute in order to ascertain what is the background policy to the statute. The purposive approach is typical of the way in which EU law needs to be interpreted, as well as human rights legislation.

In *Jones* v *Tower Boot Co* (1997), a worker was subjected to physical and verbal racial abuse by co-workers. Under the Race Relations Act 1975, s 32 an employer was liable for any actions of an employee carried out "in the course of employment". The employer argued that it did not engage its employees in order for them to racially abuse colleagues, but to work in a factory. Therefore, the employer could not be liable for the abuse. The Court of Appeal, however, gave a wide interpretation to s 32, stating that it should be interpreted to enable it to achieve its purpose. The purpose of the law was to eliminate discrimination in the workplace and to make both employees and employers liable for acts of racial harassment. Thus, the employers were held to be liable.

The modern or unified contextual approach

A more standardised approach to statutory interpretation is developing – but the approach of individual judges in specific cases continues to range along the continuum highlighted in the purposive approach illustrated above. However, given the influence of EU law within the UK, and the enactment of the Human Rights Act 1998, the continuum has shortened. It is now very rare to use the literal rule, for example, entirely on its own. Such legislation demands to be read as a "living instrument" and within its relevant context, and part of that context is the object the legislature had in mind when enacting the legislation.

Rules of the modern approach

A number of rules have been laid out pertaining to the modern approach and these have been most authoritatively catalogued by Cross in his seminal work on *Statutory Interpretation* (3rd edn, 1995) as follows:

(1) the court must give effect to the grammatical, ordinary, or technical meaning of words within the general context of the statute;

(2) if the court considers that giving such effect would produce an outcome which is contrary to the purpose of the statute, then any secondary meaning which the words are capable of bearing may be used;

(3) in order to prevent a statutory provision from being unintelligible, absurd, unworkable, or irreconcilable with the rest of the statute, the court may read in words which it considers to be necessarily implied by words which are already in the statute and has a limited power to add to, alter or ignore any other statutory words;

(4) in applying the above rules the court may resort to specific aids to construction and presumptions (outlined further below);

(5) the court must interpret a statute so as to give effect to directly applicable EU law, and, in so far as this is not possible, must refrain from applying the statutory provisions which conflict with that law.

To Cross's original rules, one can now add a sixth:

(6) by virtue of the Human Rights Act 1998, s 3, in that so far as it is possible to do so, both primary and subordinate legislation must be read and given effect in a way which is compatible with the Convention rights.

AIDS TO STATUTORY INTERPRETATION

The modern approach to statutory interpretation allows the courts to consider both the context of the statute as well as the intention of the legislature. In order to discover the context of the statute, a court will often have to rely upon certain aids to assist interpretation. Here follows a brief guide to the various aids which may be utilised.

Intrinsic aids to statutory interpretation

Intrinsic or internal aids are found within the statute itself and can be categorised as follows:

Interpretation sections

Some statutes contain their own definitions within a specially written interpretation section. For example, in the Theft Act 1968, a statutory definition of theft is provided within the Act itself along with subsequent sections which further interpret the definition fully.

Long title

The long title to an Act of Parliament has long been held as an aid to statutory interpretation. It often contains a preamble which gives an indication as to the context of the Act itself. The short title may also be used as an indicator but, given its brevity, its usefulness as an aid is doubtful.

Preambles

Preambles ceased to be used in the 19th century, except in Private Acts of Parliament. However, they once provided a very useful contextual preamble about the mischief which the Act was intended to solve.

Headings/marginal notes

Any headings and marginal notes used within a statute may assist in interpretation.

Punctuation

Punctuation may be used as an aid in cases of ambiguity.

Other enacting words

An examination of the whole wording of a statute can give an indication of the overall purpose of the legislation. Other words or parts of a statute may indicate that a particular interpretation of that provision will lead to absurdity when taken with another section.

Explanatory notes

Such notes are a relatively new addition as an aid to statutory interpretation, having only first been published in 1999. It is now accepted authority that explanatory notes to an Act of Parliament may be used as an aid to interpretation: *R (Westminster City Council)* v *National Asylum Support Service* (2002).

Linguistic aids to statutory interpretation

The eiusdem generis *rule*

Literally meaning words of the same genus or class, this rule restricts the scope of general words to those that fall into the common genus already supplied within the statutory provision in question. For example, a statute may contain a provision which applies to "lions, tigers, leopards and other animals". The *eiusdem generis* rule would mean that "other animals" must be within the same class or genus as those preceding. Thus it may include a panther, for example, but not a sheep.

The noscitur a sociis *rule*

Literally meaning "a thing is known from its associates". Under this rule, the meaning of an ambiguous word or phrase may be interpreted from the other words or phrases surrounding it within the statute. For example, in the case of *Inland Revenue Commissioners* v *Frere* (1965), a section of an Act set out rules for "interest, annuities or other annual interest". The question arose as to whether the first word of this phrase included interest paid monthly or daily. Using *noscitur a sociis*, the court held that only interest paid annually was affected by the Act.

The expressio unius est exclusio alterius *rule*

Literally meaning "the expression of one thing is the exclusion of another". Under this rule, where there is a list of words within a statute but no general words follow after them, the statute applies only to the particular items mentioned. Thus, for example in *R* v *Inhabitants of Sedgley* (1831), the Poor Relief Act 1601 levied rates on occupiers of "lands, houses and coalmines". The specific wording and the absence of any general terms such as "other" meant that mines other than coal were specifically excluded from the remit of the Act.

Statutory presumptions

There are a number of presumptions which the courts may use to ascertain the intention of a legislature, or specifically the meaning of words within a statute. Presumptions are numerous and frequently conflict but can be categorised as follows.

Presumptions of general application

These are presumptions in the form of long-established rules which will be held to apply unless there are any indications to the contrary. For example, it is presumed that a statute does not have retrospective effect unless so stated specifically, that Parliament intends everyone to have a hearing before being deprived of a legal right, and that Parliament does not intend to impose criminal liability without *mens rea*. These are just a few examples.

Presumptions in doubtful cases

Such presumptions only apply where there is doubt as to the meaning of the statute, and they tend to reflect judicial policies which have been built up over the years. There is no definitive list of these presumptions and they often tend to centre around the relationship between the courts and Parliament. Some examples are the presumption that Parliament does not intend to alter the common law unless expressly stated by the Act of Parliament, the presumption of the supremacy of Parliament, and the presumption that Parliament does not intend to interfere with vested rights or to make statutes operate retrospectively.

Extrinsic aids to statutory interpretation

Extrinsic or external aids to statutory interpretation consist of anything which cannot be found within the statute itself but may assist in ascertaining the context of the statute. They can be categorised as follows:

Dictionaries

Notable dictionaries of the time, for example the *Oxford English Dictionary*, may be used to ascertain the meaning of a word within a statute.

Earlier statutes

These can include previous statutes dealing with the same or similar areas of law and the Interpretation Act 1978 which lists common statutory definitions.

Previous decisions

Earlier precedent may be relied upon to assist interpretation.

Other statutes

Statutes *in pari materia* (on the same subject-matter) may be used to assist interpretation.

Legislative history

The courts may examine, for example, what defect in the common law Parliament was attempting to resolve in passing the statute.

Government publications

Government publications which precede and lead to the passing of the statute in question may be used to assist interpretation. These include the Reports of Royal Commissions, Law Commissions, and government departmental reports, etc They have become acceptable extrinsic aids since the decision in *Black-Clawson International Ltd* v *Papierwerke Waldhof-Aschaffenburg AG* (1975).

Hansard/Parliamentary Debates – the rule in Pepper v Hart

Hansard consists of the official daily reports of the debates held in Parliamentary proceedings. Until the House of Lords' decision in *Pepper (Inspector of Taxes)* v *Hart* (1993), references to *Hansard* in statutory interpretation were excluded, and, indeed, considered to be a breach of parliamentary privilege. However, the rule in *Pepper* permits *Hansard* to be used only in fairly specific circumstances:

- the legislation must be ambiguous, obscure or lead to an absurdity;
- the material relied upon consists of a clear statement made by a Minister or other promoter of the Bill made in Parliament and would clearly resolve the ambiguity, obscurity, or absurdity; and
- *Hansard* cannot be used to find the primary meaning of words, or to look at the Parliamentary debate as a whole.

However, in some cases the courts seem to have relaxed the circumstances. See for example, *Warwickshire County Council* v *Johnson* (1993).

Essential Facts

- Often a term or a provision contained within a statute will be unclear or ambiguous and this may require the court to interpret the precise meaning of the term or provisions. In doing so the court should attempt to ascertain what the intention of the legislature was in passing the statute.
- The three traditional rules of statutory interpretation consist of the literal rule, the golden rule and the mischief rule.
- The modern approaches to statutory interpretation consist of the purposive approach and the modern or unified contextual approach.
- There are a number of aids which the court may use to assist in interpreting a statute. These are categorised as intrinsic aids, extrinsic aids, linguistic aids, and presumptions.
- The rule in the decision of *Pepper (Inspector of Taxes)* v *Hart* (1993) allowed the reports of *Hansard* to be used as an extrinsic aid to statutory interpretation.

Essential Cases

Pepper (Inspector of Taxes) v Hart (1993): teachers at a private school had their children educated at a concessionary rate. They appealed against the basis of a tax decision. The relevant legislation was ambiguous. The House of Lords held that parliamentary material may be referred to as an aid to statutory interpretation where "(a) legislation is ambiguous or obscure, or leads to an absurdity; (b) the material relied upon consists of one or more statements by a Minister or other promoter of the Bill together if necessary with such other Parliamentary material as is necessary to understand such statements and their effect; (c) the statements relied upon are clear" (Lord Browne-Wilkinson, at 640).

Further Reading

- R Cross, J Bell and G Engle, *Statutory Interpretation* (3rd edn, 1995).
- F A R Bennion, *Bennion on Statutory Interpretation* (6th edn, 2013).

6 INTRODUCTION TO CASE LAW AND JUDICIAL PRECEDENT

JUDICIAL PRECEDENT

Judicial precedent is the most important source of law after legislation. It is sometimes also known as case law, or common law. Precedent is not created by Parliament; instead, it emanates from the decisions of judges in cases heard before them.

As such, precedent can often be difficult to find and interpret since it must be extracted from the written judgment of cases. With legislation, many drafters are involved in creating the most precise wording and form possible to avoid any ambiguities. However, judges will often produce their decisions in various styles, and some more clearly than others. Nonetheless, when a precedent is extracted from a case it forms part of the body of law in that area and can be regarded as authoritative.

The relationship between precedent and legislation is an important one and worthy of note. Since legislation is the most important source of law, its position is supreme. Through the doctrine of the supremacy of Parliament, legislation cannot be altered by any kind of judicial precedent. Conversely, it is possible for legislation to alter precedent. For example, Parliament may decide to legislate for an area which has been traditionally governed by common law and the law of precedent. In England and Wales, for example, the Theft Act 1968 codified the common law of theft. This meant that the Theft Act superseded the pre-existing common law in that area.

The rules of precedent

Judicial precedent operates under the principle of *stare decisis* which literally means "to stand by decisions". This principle means that a court must follow and apply the law as set out in the decisions of higher courts in previous cases. In this way a consistent body of precedent can be created and applied with some certainty. But not all precedents are binding, and there are a number of rules which are applied by the judiciary in ascertaining the status of a precedent.

If a precedent is to be followed by a judge in a current case, then first it must be "in point". This means that the question of law answered in the previous case must be the same as the question before the current judge.

It is not the facts of the case which must be similar but the actual point of law being dealt with in relation to those facts.

In deciding whether a precedent is "in point", a judge needs to identify the *ratio decidendi* of the original decision. The *ratio* is the point of law which led to the decision. Sometimes judges will make it clear what the reason for the decision was in a case, by clearly stating so. More often, however, they will not and thus finding the *ratio* of a precedent can be a difficult task.

There may also be statements made in a case which are *obiter dicta*, meaning "things said by the way". These do not form part of the reasoning for the decision or part of the *ratio*. They are often hypothetical questions or issues which illustrate how different facts in the case could lead to a different decision. *Obiter* remarks are never binding; they are merely persuasive on a judge. Their degree of persuasiveness will depend upon the authority of the judge who made the remarks.

If a precedent is not "in point" then it becomes merely "persuasive". A precedent which is persuasive is not binding upon a judge and it may be distinguished. If a judge decides to distinguish a precedent then he is not bound to follow it. This leads to the development of the law in dealing with new situations. On the other hand, if a precedent is "in point", then it may be binding and the judge will be obliged to follow and apply the *ratio* of that decision. Yet this is ultimately dependent upon the position of the court within the hierarchy.

Precedent and the court hierarchy

It is not simply enough that a precedent be "in point" in order for it to be binding. The relationship between the court where a precedent originated from and that of the court making the current decision is also crucial. As a general rule, in Scots law, a court will only be bound to follow the precedent of a court of higher status. Decisions from courts with lower status are, as a rule, only persuasive. Precedents from courts outwith Scotland can also be considered but, apart from decisions of the Supreme Court, none of these precedents is binding. On matters of EU law, all UK courts are bound by precedents of the European Court of Justice. Here follows a brief overview of the principles of *stare decisis* in operation:

Criminal courts

- The *Justice of the Peace Court*, being the lowest criminal court, is bound by the decisions of the High Court of Justiciary (both as an appeal and as a trial court).

- The *Sheriff Court* is bound by the decisions of the High Court of Justiciary (both as an appeal and as a trial court).
- The *High Court of Justiciary (trial court)* is bound by the decisions of the High Court of Justiciary sitting as an appeal court. A decision of one Lord of Justiciary in the trial court does not bind another Lord of Justiciary in the trial court.
- The *High Court of Justiciary (appeal court)*, being the highest and most authoritative of the criminal courts, is not bound by its own precedents. However, any precedent which was questioned would have to be reviewed by a larger number of judges. A Full Bench of judges could easily overrule a precedent set by three appeal court judges.

Civil courts

- The *Sheriff Court*, being the lowest civil court, is bound by the decisions of the Inner House of the Court of Session and by the decisions of the Supreme Court in Scottish appeals. A decision by one sheriff does not bind another sheriff, although sheriffs are bound by the sheriffs principal of that sheriffdom. A decision by a sheriff principal does not bind another sheriff principal.
- The *Court of Session (Outer House)* is bound by the decisions of the Supreme Court in Scottish appeals and by decisions of seven or more judges. Lords Ordinary are also bound by decisions of the Inner House of the Court of Session. The decision of a Lord Ordinary in the Outer House does not bind another Lord Ordinary in the Outer House.
- The *Court of Session (Inner House)* is bound by the decisions of the Supreme Court in Scottish appeals. Either Division, or an Extra Division of the Inner House, is bound by its own previous decisions. Any precedent called into question can be overruled by a Full Bench of judges.
- The *Supreme Court of the United Kingdom* sits as a final court of appeal in Scottish civil matters. Decisions of the Supreme Court are binding on all Scottish civil courts. The Court normally considers itself to be bound by its own precedents but may depart from them when circumstances dictate. In relation to devolution matters, the Court is not bound by its own precedents but they are binding in *all* other legal proceedings.

The House of Lords and the Privy Council

Historically, the Appellate Committee of the House of Lords served as the final court of appeal in Scottish civil cases. Under s 98 of and Sch 6 to the Scotland Act 1998, the Judicial Committee of the Privy Council considered "devolution issues" in both civil and criminal cases. Since October 2009, under Pt 3 of the Constitutional Reform Act 2005, the Supreme Court replaced the Appellate Committee of the House of Lords and took over the devolution issue jurisdiction of the Judicial Committee of the Privy Council.

SCOTTISH CRIMINAL COURTS

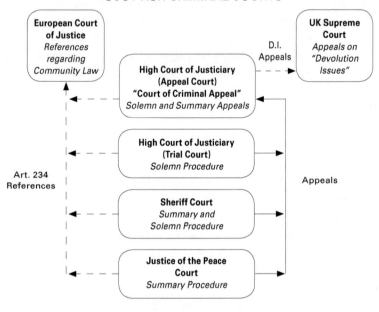

SCOTTISH CIVIL COURTS

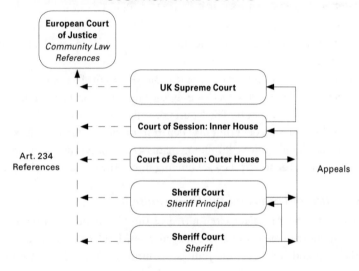

LAW REPORTING AND SOURCES OF CASE LAW

In order for the principle of *stare decisis* to operate, a judge must know what the previous decisions of courts are. Case reports, or "law reports", make this possible. Although earlier collections of cases exist, it was in the 19th century that a formalised system of law reporting was established in Scotland and England. There are currently many different series of law reports published, which reproduce judgments and add supplementary information by an editor. It may take some time between a judgment being handed down and its being published as a report. Similar systems of law reporting operate in other common law jurisdictions.

Sources of case law

Reported cases

Not all cases are reported. Indeed, given the volume of cases passing through the courts, only a small minority of cases are reported.

Whether a case is reported is decided by the editor of a series of reports. Generally speaking, to merit reporting a case must introduce a new legal principle or rule, modify an existing principle or settle a doubtful question of law. A case may be reported if it addresses an issue of statutory interpretation or illustrates a new application of an accepted principle.

It is most often the decisions of the superior courts which are reported, but in a small jurisdiction, such as Scotland, the decisions of lower courts are commonly reported.

Digests

A digest is a publication which contains summaries of cases. Digests can be a useful way of finding and checking the status of a case. They may also be the only source of a case available to you – especially if the case remains unreported. Examples include *The Faculty Digest* and *Shaw's Digest*, which contain information about older Scottish cases, and *The Digest: annotated British, Commonwealth and European cases*. The *Current Law Year Book* and *Monthly Digest* also contain summaries of cases.

Transcripts

Transcripts of judgments are documents produced by a court (or reproduced by a publisher) which contain the opinion of the judge(s) with no additional information added. If a case remains unreported, a transcript may be the only source of the judgment. For some cases an application to the court which heard the case is the only method of obtaining a transcript. However, many transcripts are now made available electronically through public access and subscription services. Given the delay in reporting, such services have become an increasingly important source of recent judgments.

Different series of law reports

There are many different series of law reports and a case may be reported in more than one series. Some series are given more authority than others by courts and in academic writing. Reports are usually published in weekly, monthly or bi-monthly parts throughout the year and subsequently bound into one or more volumes for each year.

Principal Scottish series

Session Cases begins in 1821 and contains reports of cases from the Scottish superior courts. Each volume of *Session Cases* is divided into separate sections reflecting the different courts. These are currently: *UK Supreme Court Cases*, *Justiciary Cases* and *Court of Session Cases* (older volumes include *Privy Council Cases* and *House of Lords Cases* sections). Each section is independently paginated (ie they all begin at page 1). This series is authoritative: there are practice notes from the Court of Session and High Court of Justiciary stating that when a case is reported in the *Session Cases* or *Justiciary Cases* it must be cited from that source.

Volumes of *Session Cases* up to 1906 are referred to by the name of the general editor for that period (*Shaw*, *Dunlop*, *Macpherson*, *Rettie* and *Fraser*) and volume number.

Scots Law Times (SLT) is the other major Scottish series and begins in 1893. It reports cases from superior and other courts. SLT is divided into separate sections reflecting the different courts. These are: *Reports* (from the superior courts), *Sheriff* (from the sheriff court), *Land* (Scottish Land Court and Lands Tribunal for Scotland), and *Lyon* (Court of the Lord Lyon). In addition, SLT includes a *News* section which contains articles and current awareness items – this section is similar to a legal journal. Each section is independently paginated. From 1989 SLT has been published as two volumes, one containing the *Reports* section and the other containing the remaining sections.

Scottish Civil Law Reports begins in 1987 and contains reports from the Scottish civil courts.

Scottish Criminal Case Reports begins in 1981 and contains reports of criminal cases from the High Court and the sheriff court.

Green's Weekly Digest begins in 1986. While technically a digest rather than a series of law reports, it contains cases from superior and sheriff courts, some of which are subsequently reported more fully elsewhere.

Older cases There are various series of older Scottish law reports including *The Scottish Law Reporter* (1865–1924) and *Morison's Dictionary of Decisions* (1540–1808). *Morison's Dictionary* is a collection of cases arranged by subject rather than chronologically.

Principal English series

The Law Reports begins in 1865. It is the most authoritative English series and English practice directions state that when a case is reported in *The Law Reports* it should be cited from that source. It contains reports from the English High Court, Court of Appeal, Privy Council, UK Supreme Court and, formerly, the House of Lords. *The Law Reports* is divided into separate series, which reflect the divisions of the English High Court. Currently these series are: *Appeal Cases* (which contains UK Supreme Court and Privy Council cases), *Chancery*, *Family* and *Queen's Bench*.

The Weekly Law Reports begins in 1953. It contains reports from the English superior and appellate courts. Cases are reported more quickly than they are in *The Law Reports*.

It is published weekly and divided into three volumes for each year: volume 1 contains cases which do not merit publication in *The Law Reports*; volumes 2 and 3 (January–June and July–December respectively) contain cases which will subsequently be published in *The Law Reports*.

The All England Law Reports begins in 1936. It contains reports from the English superior and appellate courts. It is published weekly and now divided into four volumes for each year. The *All England Law Reports Reprint* contains reprints of selected cases from period 1558 to 1935.

The English Reports reproduces the many series of "nominate" reports produced up to 1873 (these were known by the *name* of their reporter, eg *Simmons*). It consists of 178 volumes. To find a report in the printed *English Reports*, you must use a table to match the volume of the nominate report to the volume of the *English Reports*: for example, volumes 1–3 of *Simmons' Reports* are found in volume 57 of the *English Reports*. The *English Reports* are available on *Westlaw, Hein Online, Justis*, and on microfilm and CD.

European series
European Court of Justice cases may be reported in other UK general or specialist reports. However, those with specific coverage of the ECJ include *The European Court Reports* and *Common Market Law Reports*.

Similarly, European Court of Human Rights cases may be reported in other series. However, series devoted to the court include *Reports of Judgments and Decisions* (formerly *European Court of Human Rights Series A: Judgments and Decisions*) and *European Human Rights Reports*.

Specialist series
There are many specialist series which contain cases on particular subjects. Examples include *Lloyd's Law Reports: Medical, Building Law Reports, Green's Family Law Reports* and *Green's Reparation Law Reports*.

Essential Facts

- Judicial precedent is the second most important source of law in the UK.
- Utilising the rules of precedent and the doctrine of *stare decisis*, court decisions become a source of law by building up a body of binding decisions.
- The *ratio decidendi* is the legal principle upon which a case is decided.
- Superior courts generally bind inferior courts but decisions only become binding if a case is "in point" and a previously decided *ratio decidendi* is the same as the *ratio* in the present case.
- Hypothetical comments made in a decision are said to be made "by the way" or *obiter dicta*. They are not binding upon future cases and are merely persuasive.
- Case law can be found in law reports, case digests and official transcripts. There are many series of law reports – the most authoritative Scottish series are *Session Cases* and *Justiciary Cases*.

Further Reading

- B Clark and G Keegan, *Scottish Legal System Essentials* (3rd edn, 2012), Chapters 2 and 3.
- F Grant, *Legal Research Skills for Scots Lawyers* (3rd edn, 2014), Chapter 3.
- G Holborn, *Butterworths Legal Research Guide* (2nd edn, 2001), Chapter 5.

7 FINDING AND USING CASE LAW

Case law, like legislation, can change over time. Just because a decision was good law once does not mean it remains so today. A lawyer needs to be able not only to find and read case law, but also to be able to check whether it has been subject to subsequent judicial consideration and whether it remains good law.

Here, we look at how a case may be judicially considered, the structure of a law report, and how to find and check the status of case law.

JUDICIAL CONSIDERATION OF PREVIOUS DECISIONS

A court in handing down a judgment may consider a previous decision in several ways. A previous decision may be:

- *Approved* – a higher court may state that *another* case heard by a lower court was correctly decided.
- *Applied* – a court may apply the reasoning of a previous case in a current case, where the facts are different from those of the previous case.
- *Followed* – a court may be bound by a previous decision where the material facts were substantially the same as in the instant case.
- *Distinguished* – a court may not follow a previous and otherwise binding decision because there is a difference in, for example, the material facts. The previous case remains good law.
- *Disapproved* – a higher court may state that *another* case heard by a lower court was wrongly decided. The court indicates that the previous case may not be good law – but does not expressly overrule it.
- *Doubted* – a court while not expressly overruling a previous case may give reasons to show that it may have been wrongly decided.
- *Not followed* – a court may choose not to follow the decision of a court of co-ordinate jurisdiction where the material facts were substantially the same as the instant case.
- *Overruled* – a court may expressly overrule the *ratio decidendi* of an inferior court's decision in *another* case.

In addition, if a case is appealed to a higher court, the decision of the lower court may be:

- *Affirmed* – the *same* case is held to have been correctly decided by the lower court. It is good law.
- *Reversed* – the *same* case is held to have been wrongly decided by the lower court. It is not good law.

Furthermore, under the doctrine of parliamentary supremacy, a decision in a case may be *superseded* by legislation.

Importantly, if a case has been reversed, overruled (or superseded by legislative provisions) it is no longer good law and should not be relied on as authority.

STRUCTURE OF A LAW REPORT

A law report is divided into distinct sections. The most important of these is the judgment, or opinion, which is the text of the judge's reasoning. However, other sections added by the editor assist in understanding the case and assessing its likely impact. Sections usually found in a report are:

- *parties' names* – the parties involved in the case;
- *court* – the court before which the case was heard;
- *date of hearing* – often some time before it is reported;
- *name of judge* – the judge(s) who heard the case;
- *subject-matter of the case* – a list of keywords or subject terms;
- *headnote (rubric)* – a summary of the case outlining the material facts, legal issues and decision;
- *judicial history* – details of the case's history (in inferior courts);
- *authorities referred to* – a list of cases, legislation and textbooks referred to in the case;
- *opinion of the court* – the judge's decision and reasoning. Judgments of superior courts are now divided into numbered paragraphs for ease of reference (numbers are in square brackets, eg [9]);
- *outcome*;
- *representation* – the solicitors and advocates (or barristers) who represented the parties.

WHERE TO FIND CASE LAW

Print sources

Printed series of law reports as well as digest works are held by most law libraries. In addition, many cases are summarised or excerpts are reproduced in "cases and materials" books on a subject.

Online subscription services

A number of subscription services contain not only full-text reproductions of law reports but also summaries and transcripts of cases. There is much overlap in the series covered by different services though some reports are available on one and not on another. If looking for a particular report of a case you may need to check several services.

Westlaw Among the many series of reports available are: *Session Cases* (1898–), *Scots Law Times* (1909–), *The Law Reports* (1865–), *The Weekly Law Reports* (1953–)and *The English Reports* (1220–1865). *Westlaw* also contains transcripts of some unreported cases. In addition, summaries of many cases are available in the form of "case analyses".

Lexis®Library Among the many series of case reports available are: *Session Cases* (1930–), *Scottish Civil Law Reports* (1986–), and *Scottish Criminal Case Reports* (1981–); *The Law Reports* (1865–), *The Weekly Law Reports* (1953–)and *All England Law Reports* (1936–). *Lexis®Library* also contains transcripts of some unreported cases and summaries of some cases.

Justis Content includes: *Session Cases* (1821–), *The Law Reports* (1865–), *The Weekly Law Reports* (1953–) and *The English Reports* (1220–1873).

Lawtel Transcripts of many judgments are available on *Lawtel*.

HeinOnline *The English Reports* are available on *HeinOnline* (1220–1865).

Websites

Scottish Court Service (http://www.scotcourts.gov.uk/) This site provides access to transcripts of judgments from the Court of Session (1999–), High Court of Justiciary (1999–)and sheriff courts (1999–). Judgements published and hosted on the site are those which address significant points of law or are in the public interest.

UK Supreme Court (http://www.supremecourt.gov.uk/) This site contains transcripts of all judgments handed down (under "Decided Cases") from 2009 onwards. It also provides "press summaries", which outline the key points of judgments as well as video footage of the hearing and the judgment.

BAILII (http://www.bailii.org/)   The British and Irish Legal Information Institute website, although not an official source, is a comprehensive database of British and Irish primary legal material. Court of Session opinions from 1998 and selected opinions from 1879 are included. It covers courts and tribunals from throughout the UK and Ireland as well as the European Court of Justice and European Court of Human Rights.

Curia (http://curia.europa.eu/)   *"Curia"* is the official website of the European Court of Justice and provides information about, and access to, full-text judgments of the court (1997–).

Hudoc (via http://www.echr.coe.int/echr) *Hudoc* is the official database of the European Court of Human Rights and provides information about, and access to, full-text judgments of the court (1998–).

HOW TO FIND AND CHECK CASE LAW

Aids to finding and checking case law

There are a number of ways to locate case law including on official and unofficial websites (as described above – Scottish Courts website, Supreme Court website, BAILII). However, the most efficient way to check the status of case law is by using an online legal database or by traditional print methods. Online databases providing access to full-text law reports offer value-added features which make locating and checking the status of a case easy.

    Westlaw contains "Case Analysis" documents, *Lexis®Library* contains "CaseSearch" documents and *JustCite* contains case documents. These include information about where a case is reported, whether it has been judicially considered or referred to in later cases (either positively or negatively), and citations to other cases referred to in the case. *Westlaw* and *Lexis®Library* also use case status icons (signals) to indicate what kind of treatment a case has received and if it is still "good law". However, it is also useful to know how to use traditional print aids which provide a systematic and effective way of tracing the status of a case.

Current Law

The principal traditional aids to locating and checking case law are the *Current Law Case Citator*, *Year Book* and *Monthly Digest*.

    The *Case Citator* consists of a number of volumes each covering a different period. From 2005 onwards, they are published in annual volumes:

1948–1976; 1977–1997; 1988–2001; 2002–2004; 2005; 2006; 2007; 2008; etc.

Each volume contains the following information for the period covered:

- new cases with citations to reports etc; and
- instances where the decision in a case has been judicially considered in another case. (This is noted whatever the date of the original case – eg a case from 1932 applied in a case in 1975 is referred to in the 1948–1976 volume.)

The citator is divided into separate English and Scottish sections. Cases are listed alphabetically by the first party's name.

The *Current Law Year Book*'s annual volumes contain summaries of legal developments during the year – including case digests. These summaries, or "items", are grouped under subject headings. Each item is given a number, eg 5430. These are referred to in the *Case Citator* by year and item number:

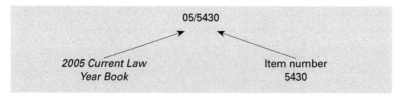

The *Current Law Monthly Digest* is, in effect, the current year's parts of the *Year Book*. Each part contains a cumulative Table of Cases reported during the current year. So the table in the December part covers the whole year. References are given to case summaries by month (part) and item number (eg **Jan** 372). This is a useful aid for locating recently reported cases.

Other digests and indexes of cases may be used to locate and check cases for the period before 1948.

Citation of cases

Modern cases are cited in the form:

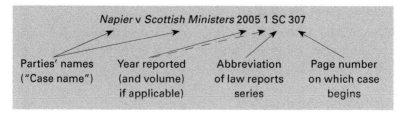

The above citation indicates that the case was reported in volume one of the 2005 *Session Cases* beginning at page 307. The year given is that of the report, not necessarily the same as that in which the case was heard.

For Scottish cases, if the year is in round brackets (2005) then it is not strictly required to locate the case as the series has consecutively numbered volumes. If the year is not in brackets then it is required to locate the case.

For English cases, if the year is in square brackets [2005] then it is required to locate the case. If the year is in round brackets (2005) then it is not strictly required to locate the case as the series has consecutively numbered volumes.

Neutral citations

To make it easier to cite and trace unreported judgments, both Scottish (since 2005) and English (since 2001), courts have begun assigning unique numbers to judgments.

Thus, cases may now be referred to by "neutral citation". These are known as media neutral citations because they are independent of published reports. Neutral citations are given in the form of:

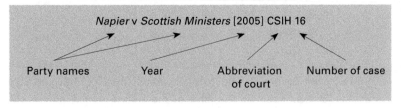

Napier v Scottish Ministers [2005] CSIH 16

Party names   Year   Abbreviation   Number of case
                       of court

Sections within the case may be referred to by paragraph number, which is shown at the end of the citation between square brackets:

Napier v Scottish Ministers [2005] CSIH 16 [20]

When citing a subsequently reported case, you should cite both and the neutral citation should precede the citation to the published report.

Finding cases by citation

Cases searches on *Westlaw*, *Lexis®Library* and other databases include the option of searching by full citation. This is often the quickest way of retrieving a case on these databases.

Identifying abbreviations

Case citations use abbreviations – in published reports for the case report series and in neutral citations for the court. There are print and online aids to help you identify these abbreviations.

Traditional methods   Abbreviations can be checked in a variety of print sources. These include the table of abbreviations for law reports and legal journals in the *Current Law Year Book* and *Monthly Digest*. Donald Raistrick's newly updated edition of *Index to Legal Citations and Abbreviations* (4th edn, 2013) includes abbreviations from law reports and legal journals and includes organisations, legal terminology and other words that are commonly abbreviated such as certain Acts of Parliament.

Online   The *Cardiff Index to Legal Abbreviations* (http://www. legalabbrevs.cardiff.ac.uk/) is a freely available web-based service that is widely used. You can search by abbreviation to find the full name, or search by full name for the accepted (preferred) abbreviation. Coverage includes reported cases, neutral citations, journals and some legislative publications and major textbooks. UK and non-UK jurisdictions are covered.

Once you know what the abbreviation means, you can locate the report by series, year (or volume) and page.

Finding cases by party names

Traditional methods

If you only have the names of the parties you will first need to find out the citation. This can be done by looking up the case by first named party in the *Current Law Case Citator.*

If you do not know the year in which the case was reported, you will need to check all volumes. If you know the year, you can go directly to the volume covering the relevant period; alternatively, you can look up the table of cases in the appropriate volume of the *Current Law Year Book*.

For cases within the last year, you may need to check the table of cases in the most recent volume of the *Current Law Monthly Digest*.

For cases reported before 1948 (and not judicially considered since) you will need to check other indexes and digests.

Online

Westlaw   In a "Cases" search screen, enter either or both names in the "Party Names" field. The search is not caes sensitive so you do not need to worry about capitalisation or punctuation. Results include links to a "Case Analysis" document containing details of where a case is reported. There are links to the full text of a report or transcript if it is available on

Westlaw. If the full text is not available in *Westlaw*, you can try another database, like *Lexis®Library* or get the print copy.

Lexis®Library   In the "Cases" search screen, enter party name in the "Case name" field. Search results list summaries and links to full-text cases.

Lawtel   In the "Cases" search screen, search by "Case Name" for summaries and transcripts of judgments.

Justis/JustCite   In the *Justis* "Cases" search screen, enter terms in the "Parties" fields. Search results list cases available on *Justis*. The *JustCite* "Cases" search also provides "Parties" fields. Search results provide links to sources of full-text cases.

Finding cases by subject

Traditional methods

Using the *Current Law Year Book*, look up case summaries under either the general subject headings or the index. Each annual volume needs to be checked to separately. For cases within the current year use parts of the *Current Law Monthly Digest*.

Digest works may be referred to in a similar way. *Green's Weekly Digest* is particularly useful in a Scottish context.

A textbook or encyclopaedia on a relevant subject should also make reference to the most important cases concerning that area of law.

Online

Westlaw   In a "Cases" basic search, enter words or phrases in the "Free Text" field to match against terms in the case record. Results can be filtered by adding another term to search within the results or by topic, court, jurisdiction or status. The advanced search gives more options to help focus your search – by using subject headings. These are assigned to cases in the database and describe the main focus of the case. You can choose from a list.

Lexis®Library   In a "Cases" search, enter terms in the general "Search terms" field. *Lexis* also has a "Summary" field for specifying "catchwords" and "headnote" terms. This is similar to the subject heading search in Westlaw and should be a more focused search as you are matching against specific fields in the case record.

Lawtel   In a "Case Law" search, enter terms in the "Free Text" or "Keywords" fields, or select terms from the "Subject" list.

Justis/JustCite   In the *Justis* "Cases" search screen, enter terms in "Full Text", "Subject" or "Headnote" fields. The *JustCite* "Cases" search provides a "Subject" field.

Checking a case's status

Traditional and online sources may be used to check whether a case has been subsequently judicially considered and whether it is still good law.

Traditional methods

Using the *Current Law Case Citator*, look up the case alphabetically by first party name. Begin with the volume covering the year in which the case was reported, and then continue with each volume to present (or until you find the decision overruled or reversed). If the case has been considered, this will be noted beside the case name. The way in which the case has been considered (eg overruled, approved, etc) is given together with a reference to the subsequent case in the *Current Law Year Book* (eg 05/5430). To find details of the subsequent case, go to the relevant item in the *Current Law Year Book*.

Online

Westlaw   A "Case Analysis" document for a given case includes "Appellate History" and "Cases Citing" headings. Information under these headings indicates in what way a case has been subsequently considered. Cases which have been given negative consideration (eg overruled or reversed) should also be indicated with a small red "no entry" icon.

Lexis®Library   A "CaseSearch" document includes a "Case History" and "Cases referring to this case" headings. Information under these headings indicates in what way a case has been considered. Cases which have been given negative consideration should also be indicated with a small red icon with a white cross (x) in it.

JustCite   *JustCite* case documents provide information about subsequent judicial consideration under the "Subsequent Cases" heading. The *JustCite* "Subsequent Cases" tab is also available in *Justis* cases documents.

Essential Facts

- Case law can change over time through subsequent judicial consideration. Importantly, if a case is overruled or reversed by a later decision, or is superseded by legislation, it ceases to be good law.
- Volumes of printed law reports and digests can be found in libraries. Law reports, case summaries and transcripts can also be found on a number of subscription and public access online services.
- To find case law you can use the search functions on database services or the *Current Law* service.
- To check whether a case has been given subsequent judicial consideration you can use *Westlaw* "Case Analysis" documents, *Lexis®Library* "CaseSearch" documents, *JustCite*, or the *Current Law Case Citator* and *Year Book*.

Essential Abbreviations

- Up to 1906 *Session Cases* are referred to by editor:

S	Shaw
D	Dunlop
M	Macpherson
R	Rettie
F	Fraser

- Sections in *Session Cases* are referred to separately:

SC (UKSC)	UK Supreme Court
SC (HL)	House of Lords
SC (PC)	Privy Council
JC	Justiciary Cases
SC	Court of Session Cases

- Sections in *Scots Law Times* also have separate abbreviations:

SLT	Reports (from superior courts)
SLT (Sh Ct)	Sheriff Court Reports
SLT (Land Ct)	Land Court Reports

SLT (Land Tr)   Lands Tribunal Reports
SLT (Lyon)   Lyon Court Reports
SLT (Notes)   Notes of recent decisions
SLT (News)   News section

- *The Law Reports* are referred to by division:

AC   Appeal Cases
Ch   Chancery Division
Fam   Family Division
QB/KB   Queen's Bench/King's Bench

- Abbreviations used in neutral citations include:

HCJT   High Court of Justiciary (trial court)
HCJAC   High Court of Justiciary (appeal court)
CSOH   Outer House of the Court of Session
CSIH   Inner House of the Court of Session
UKSC   Supreme Court of the United Kingdom
UKHL   House of Lords
UKPC   Privy Council
EWCA Civ   Court of Appeal: Civil Division (E&W)
EWCA Crim   Court of Appeal: Criminal Division (E&W)
EWHC (QB)   High Court: Queen's Bench division (E&W)
EWHC (Fam)   High Court: Family Division (E&W)

Essential Practice Notes

Court of Session Practice Note No 5 of 2004

(available via http://www.scotcourts.gov.uk/session/practiceNotes/index.asp)

This practice note gives guidance on the neutral citation of opinions from the Court of Session:

Court of Session, Outer House: [2005] CSOH 1

Court of Session, Inner House: [2005] CSIH 1

The note also reaffirms that where a case has been reported in *Session Cases* it must be cited from that source and that other series of reports may only be used when a case is not reported in *Session Cases*.

High Court of Justiciary Practice Note No 2 of 2004

(available via http://www.scotcourts.gov.uk/justiciary/practicenotes/index.asp)

This practice note gives guidance on the neutral citation of opinions from the High Court of Justiciary:

> High Court of Justicary: [2005] HCJT 1
>
> Court of Criminal Appeal: [2005] HCJAC 1

The note also reaffirms that where a case has been reported in *Justiciary Cases* it must be cited from that source and that other series of reports may only be used when a case is not reported in *Justiciary Cases*.

Further Reading

- F Grant, *Legal Research Skills for Scots Lawyers* (3rd edn, 2014), Chapters 3 and 4.
- J Knowles, *Effective Legal Research* (4th edn, 2016), Chapter 3.
- G Holborn, *Butterworths Legal Research Guide* (2nd edn, 2001), Chapter 5.

8 INTRODUCTION TO EUROPEAN AND INTERNATIONAL SOURCES

EUROPEAN UNION LAW

European Union (EU) law has become increasingly important in the UK. As a result of its membership of the European Union, the UK has agreed to be bound by EU law. The European Communities Act 1972 ensures the applicability of EU law in the UK and states that all directly effective EU legislation creates an enforceable right within the UK and must be enforced by all courts and tribunals. It also states that all UK law must be applied subject to EU law. Therefore, EU law overarches our system of national law and, if there is any conflict, it is EU law which prevails.

These provisions are fairly revolutionary in that they fundamentally undermine the concept of parliamentary sovereignty and the supremacy of the UK Parliament. The implications of the European Communities Act 1972 were discussed in great detail in the case of *R v Secretary of State for Transport, ex parte Factortame (No 2)*. On appeal, it was affirmed by the House of Lords that an Act of Parliament contradicting EU legislation could not be enforced in the courts of the UK. Furthermore, since EU law had to be enforced, courts were entitled to issue orders to such effect. In effect, the 1972 Act allows EU legislation to take precedence over that of the UK. There have been many positive effects of this principle, and some areas of UK law have been fundamentally changed for the better due to the influence of EU law.

Sources of EU law

Primary sources of EU law comprise legislation and case law. Secondary sources of legal information include journals, textbooks, and encyclopaedias. EU official publications include policy and pre-legislative documents. The focus here is on the primary sources of EU law. General EU legal information can be found from sources including:

- *Europa* (http://europa.eu/) – the official EU website. In addition to legislation and case law, *Europa* contains statistical information, information about EU policies and activities, and EU press releases.
- *European Current Law* – a print service which is published monthly and consolidated annually into the *European Current Law Year Book*. The service includes information about developments in EU legislation and case law.

EU LEGISLATION

EU primary legislation: Treaties

Primary legislation consists of the Treaties which originally established the European Economic Community (EEC) and subsequently amended and altered its constitution. Since the EEC was created in 1957 it has greatly developed and expanded in its form and membership, becoming the European Community (EC) and now the European Union (EU). Upon joining the EU, Member States agree to be bound by the provisions of the Treaties. It is through the authority of the Treaties that secondary legislation is created. Some of the key European Treaties are as follows:

- the *Treaties of Rome 1957* led to the creation of the European Economic Community and the European Atomic Energy Authority;
- the *Treaty of Accession 1972* marked the entry of the UK to the EEC and further enlargement through the membership of Ireland and Denmark;
- the *Maastricht Treaty 1992* created the European Union;
- the *Amsterdam Treaty 1997* set new objectives for the European Union;
- the *Treaty of Nice 2001* saw the creation of the EU Charter of Fundamental Rights;
- the *Treaty of Lisbon 2007*, altered the workings and constitutional framework of the European Union.

EU secondary legislation

Secondary legislation consists of Regulations, Directives, Decisions and Recommendations and Opinions.

Regulations are of general application and become law within all Member States automatically. Member States do not have to pass any national legislation to apply the Regulations and they supersede any national law. Such Regulations are described as having "direct effect" within the Member States.

Directives on the other hand, state objectives to be achieved by Member States and it is up to each individual state to enact or amend national legislation in order to comply. A Directive does not, therefore, have direct applicability. There is normally a time limit within which a Directive must be implemented. UK implementation is often by SI, but may be by statute. If a Directive is sufficiently clear and specific, and if the time limit for implementation has elapsed, then the Directive will have direct effect.

This means that a citizen can rely on the Directive to challenge the failure of the UK Government to comply.

Decisions are issued by the European Commission. The Commission is the administrative body of the EU and is responsible for all aspects of decision-making within the EU. The Commission ensures that Member States uphold their obligations to implement EU laws. Failure to implement obligations can result in enforcement proceedings being taken against a Member State. This involves the Commission investigating an alleged breach and issuing a reasoned opinion or decision on the matter. Decisions are binding upon the state to whom they are addressed and may also be issued to a public body, a private company or an individual.

Recommendations and Opinions have no binding force.

Structure of a Directive or Regulation

The main constituent parts of a Directive or Regulation are:

- *Title* – includes institutional origin, date of adoption, and Directive/Regulation number, eg *Directive 95/46/EC of the European Parliament and of the Council of 24 October 1995 on the protection of individuals with regard to the processing of personal data and on the free movement of such data.*
- *Enacting authority* – ie Commission, Council, Parliament and Council.
- *Treaty basis* – treaty and article, eg "Having regard to the Treaty establishing the European Community, and in particular Article 137(2) thereof".
- *Legislative procedure* – eg "Having regard to the proposal from the Commission, Having regard to the opinion of the European Economic and Social Committee, Having consulted the Committee of the Regions, Acting in accordance with the procedure referred to in Article 251 of the Treaty".
- *Recitals* – preliminary statements explaining the background to the legislation (recitals begin "Whereas ...").
- *Articles* – contain the substantive provisions of the Directive/Regulation. Articles are subdivided into paragraphs.
- *Entry into force provisions* – an article towards the end of the Directive/Regulation contains provisions for when it shall enter into force.
- *Annexes* – analogous to Schedules in UK statutes.

WHERE TO FIND EU LEGISLATION

Print sources

Official Journal of the European Union The *Official Journal* (*OJ*) contains the official authoritative version of legislation. The *OJ* is comprised of different series; the two you are most likely to encounter are:

- *"L" series* – contains practically all secondary legislation adopted;
- *"C" series* – contains a variety of "information and notices" including proposed legislation and announcements of court proceedings. The text of treaties may appear here (eg Treaty of Nice, OJ 2001 C80/1).

The text of legislation is not consolidated; it appears as it was when adopted and does not reflect subsequent amendments or revocations.

The *OJ* is available online on *EUR-lex* (1952– ; in English 1973–). From the homepage (http://eur-lex.europa.eu/homepage.html) choose the tab for the Official Journal.

Encyclopedia of European Union Law   This looseleaf encyclopaedia contains EU constitutional texts, including treaties, other agreements and ancillary texts.

Encyclopedia of European Community Law   This looseleaf encyclopaedia contains in force, consolidated (revised) and annotated EU secondary legislation.

Other collections   The *Avizandum* and *Blackstone's* statute collections contain consolidated EU legislation relevant to each title's subject area. Other subject specific encyclopaedic works also contain relevant EU legislation.

Websites

EUR-Lex (http://eur-lex.europa.eu/)   *EUR-Lex* provides access to European Union law, including:

- OJ (electronic copies of all Official Journals 1952– ; in English 1973–). From 1 July 2013, the electronic editions of the OJ have legal effect (and the paper version ceases to have legal effect – see Regulation (EU) No 216/2013);
- EU law (EU treaties, directives, regulations, decisions, consolidated legislation, etc);

- preparatory acts (legislative proposals, reports, green and white papers, etc); and
- international agreements.

You can browse or search for legislation.

Online subscription services

Westlaw   Content includes primary legislation (1951–) and secondary legislation as it appears in the *OJ* "L" series (1952–). Legislation can be searched or browsed by following the link to the "EU" search screen from the *Westlaw UK* homepage.

Lexis®Library   Content includes consolidated primary and secondary legislation. To access EU legislation, follow the link to the "Legislation" search screen, then the link to "International Legislation". From the "International Legislation" search screen, search or browse secondary legislation by selecting "EU legislation" from the drop-down "sources" menu (for primary legislation and other treaties, select "EU treaties").

Justis EU   Content includes the text of primary and secondary legislation.

Lawtel   Content includes records of all adopted legislation since 1987 and most prior to that date. Links to the full text of legislation as published in the *OJ* are provided. To search EU material, from the *Lawtel* homepage, under the "Specialist Areas" tab follow the link to "EU".

HOW TO FIND AND CHECK EU LEGISLATION

Aids to finding and checking EU legislation

Some online services which provide access to EU legislation have functions which help in locating and checking the legislation's status. *EUR-Lex* (http://eur-lex.europa.eu/homepage.html) records include sections "About this document" and "Linked documents" giving information about current status. *Westlaw* and *Justis EU* legislation documents and *Lawtel* records provide similar information.

"Traditional" printed aids include the following.

Index to the Official Journal of the EU   The annual index comprises an alphabetical index and a methodological t+able.

Directory of European Union Legislation   Available via *EUR-Lex* (under the "More" tab), this directory classifies legislation by subject, listing any amendments. It includes links to full-text legislation.

Halsbury's Statutory Instruments: EC Legislation Implementator   Indicates if Directives have been implemented by domestic legislation in England and Wales. **NB** Scotland is not covered. (Available in print or online the *Lexis®Library* database.)

Citation of EU legislation

In January 2015, the numbering of EU legislation was harmonised to make accessing EU law easier. All legislation is now given a simple three-part number: (domain) YYYY/N, independent of the type of document. The domain (eg EU) is placed in brackets, year of publication is given in four digits and the number is sequential (starting at 1 in each year). Our first example below is the eleventh piece of legislation published in 2016.

Secondary legislation may be cited by full title:

> Commission Implementing Directive (EU) 2016/11 of 5 January 2016 amending Annex II to Council Directive 2002/57/EC on the marketing of seed of oil and fibre plants
>
> Commission Regulation (EC) No 90/2005 of 20 January 2005 determining the world market price for unginned cotton

in short form:

> Commission Implementing Directive (EU) 2016/11
>
> Directive 95/88/EC Regulation (EC) 90/2005

When using the short form of citation to legislation published prior to January 2015, it is essential that the type of act is included as Decisions and Directives appear in separate numerical sequences (eg there is also a Decision 95/88/EC). Directives are usually cited in the form year/number and Regulations in the form number/year. From 1999 the full year is given; prior to 1999 the final two digits were used (ie 1995 became 95).

Citation to legislation may include the *Official Journal* citation in addition to the full title:

> Commission Implementing Directive (EU) 2016/11 of 5 January 2016 amending Annex II to Council Directive 2002/57/EC on the marketing of seed of oil and fibre plants OJ L 3, 6.1.2016, p 48–49

Colloquial titles   Directives and Regulations may be known by a popular title (eg "Data Protection Directive"). However, these often bear little relation to the formal title so are not helpful for finding legislation. When searching, use the formal title or document number. If you do not know this, you could search secondary sources using the colloquial title and find the formal reference given in footnotes.

Finding EU legislation

EUR-Lex   You can search or browse for legislation. *EUR-lex* has a quick search on the home page which searches across all document types and dates. It works best if you are doing subject or keyword searching (see Chapter 10 for effective search strategies using keywords). The "Advanced search" screen looks complicated but actually it gives you lots of options for how you want to search and is the best choice if you have partial information about the document you want. You can limit by document type, date, author or OJ reference. Alternatively, you can browse recent legislation or the *Directory of European Union Legislation* (there are links to both on the "Legislation" page under the "EU law and related documents" tab on the home page).

Westlaw   The EU search screen has "Free text", "Parties or Title", "Case or Document No." or "Publication reference" fields. Choose whatever is appropriate based on the information you already have. You can restrict your search to "Legislation" or "Treaties" by following the relevant links under the "Browse" heading (below the search fields). This opens up a new search screen which focuses your search on just that type of document.

Lexis®Library   On the "International Legislation" search screen (link on the left of the "Legislation" screen) select "EU legislation" or "EU treaties" from the "Sources" drop-down menu and enter terms in the "Search terms" box. You can also search by title, Part or schedule or Provision, if you are looking for a specific document.

Lawtel The EU "Adopted Legislation" search screen provides fields including "Summary", "Keywords" and "References".

Justis EU The search screen provides fields including "Title", "Reference", "OJ Reference", "Full Text" and "Subject".

How to check the status of secondary legislation

You may need to check whether EU legislation is currently in force, whether it has been amended, or how it has been implemented in the UK.

In force/amended?

EUR-Lex Each record in *EUR-lex* has sections called "About this document" and "Linked documents" which provide information on the dates in force and details of amendments.

Westlaw The database uses status icons to indicate the status of legislation. Repealed legislation is indicated by a red icon indicating "Superseded or Repealed" at the top of the document record. The "Dates" link provides all dates relevant to the legislation (including in force date) and the "References" link provides links to all related documents and all modifications.

Lexis®Library Legislation is consolidated to incorporate amendments and the amending legislation is listed at the beginning of the document.

Justis EU Legislation documents provide information about "date of entry into force", "date of end of validity" and references to amending legislation.

Lawtel Legislation records provide references to amending legislation under the "Amendment History" heading.

UK implementation

EUR-Lex If there are national implementing measures for EU legislation, these are listed under the "NIM" tab on the legislation record.

Westlaw Information about implementation by Member States is given under "National Measures" (as a navigaiton link on the left of the screen).

Lexis®Library   The separate "EU tracker" service tracks the implementation of legislation across Member States including the UK.

Justis EU   Legislation documents provide references to national implementation measures including UK legislation.

Lawtel   The legislation record provides details of UK implementing measures.

Halsbury's Statutory Instruments: EC Legislation Implementator (Available in hard copy and in the *Lexis®Library* database.) This indicates whether, and by what national measure, a Directive has been implemented. **NB** Covers only England and Wales.

Proposed legislation

Proposals for legislation are published as "COM documents". These are published in the *Official Journal* "C" series and can be accessed on:

- *EUR-Lex* – select "Preparatory Acts" from the "EU Law and related documents";tab;
- *Westlaw* – in the "EU" search screen, under the "Browse" heading you can restrict the search to "Preparatory Acts";
- *Lexis®Library* – in the "International Legislation" search screen, select "EU materials" from the drop-down menu and browse or search "Preparatory documents".

Information about COM documents related to adopted legislation can be found in the "'Procedure" tab on the legislation record in *EUR-Lex* or in equivalent records on subscription services. Additionally, you can follow the life cycle of a legislative proposal until the law is adopted, using the search or browse options in the "Legislative procedures" tab.

Other sources useful for tracking legislative proposals include:

- *OEIL* – *European Parliament: Legislative Observatory* tracker service (via http://www.europarl.europa.eu/oeil/).

EU CASE LAW

Case law is produced by the European Court of Justice (ECJ) and the Court of First Instance (CFI). Courts in Member States also apply EU law.

Structure of an ECJ case report

A report of an ECJ case (as found in the *European Court Reports*) is now in the form:

- *Case number* – eg C-157/03.
- *Parties' names* – eg *Commission of the European Communities* v *Kingdom of Spain.*
- *Summary of the Judgment*★ – outlines key points of the judgment.
- *Opinion of the Advocate General*★ – independent reasoned advice to the Court.
- *Judgment of the Court*★ – delivered as a single judgment.
- *Ruling.*

★**NB** The Summary of the Judgment, Opinion of the Advocate General, and the Judgment of the Court may be treated as separate documents by some databases.

Where to find ECJ case law

Print sources

European Court Reports (ECR) (1954–2011) This official series reports all cases from the ECJ and CFI from 1954. The print edition ceased in 2011 and is now officially reported online on the *EUR-lex* website. From 1990–2011 the reports were published in two parts: Part I – ECJ cases; Part II – CFI cases. Reports may be published some years after the judgment is issued.

Common Market Law Reports (CMLR) (1962–) This series includes not only significant ECJ and CFI cases but also decisions from the courts of Member States concerning EU law. (CMLR are also available in full text on *Westlaw* using a "Cases" search.)

All England Law Reports: European Cases (All ER (EC)) (1995–) This series includes significant ECJ and CFI cases arising from all Member States. (All ER (EC) is also available in full text on *Lexis*®*Library* via a "Cases" search.)

Websites

"Curia" (http://curia.europa.eu/) The ECJ website provides access to the text of Opinions of Advocates General and Judgments of the Courts (17/06/1997–). There is a basic search screen on the home page which allows you to search by party name and date, but the advanced search screen (click the icon to the right of the search button) provides much richer options for searching, including cases citing legislation and lists of cases pending.

EUR-Lex (http://eur-lex.europa.eu/)   *Eur-Lex* contains full-text Opinions and Judgments (1992–) and summaries of judgments (1954–).

BAILII (http://www.bailii.org/)   *BAILII* contains ECJ and CFI case law (1954–). Earlier judgments appear in summary form.

Online subscription services

Westlaw   The "EU" search screen provides access to case law from 1954 onwards. Opinions of the Advocates General and Judgments are treated as separate documents.

Lexis®Library   Contains case law from 1954 onwards. Opinions of the Advocates General and Judgments are treated as separate documents. Access is from the "Cases" search screen and then by selecting "International Cases".

Justis EU   Contains full-text ECJ and CFI Judgments and Opinions of the Advocates General.

Lawtel Covers ECJ/CFI case law from 1954 onwards. Limited information is available for cases before 1989. Links are provided, where available, to full-text Judgments and Opinions. To search EU material, from the *Lawtel* homepage, under the "Specialist Areas" tab, follow the link to "EU".

How to find case law from the ECJ/CFI

Citation of ECJ/CFI case law

A case citation is usually in the form:

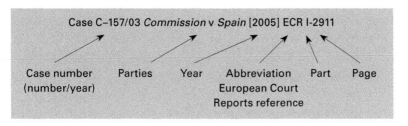

Case C–157/03 *Commission* v *Spain* [2005] ECR I-2911

| Case number (number/year) | Parties | Year | Abbreviation European Court Reports reference | Part | Page |

NB The case number refers to the year of the *application* not the year of the judgment.

Prior to 1990, ECJ case numbers had no prefix. From 1990 onwards, ECJ cases receive a "C" prefix and CFI cases a "T" prefix. A suffix "P" indicates an appeal from the CFI to the ECJ:

> Case 96/85 *Commission* v *France* [1986] ECR 1475
> Case C–157/03 *Commission* v *Spain* [2005] ECR I-2911
> Case T–177/04 *easyJet Co Ltd* v *Commission* [2006] ECR II-1931
> Case C–422/02 P *Europe Chemi-Con (Deutschland)* v *Council* [2005]
>   ECR I-791

Citation to cases from other series of reports may follow the standard citation form, eg:

> *Commission* v *Spain* (Case C–157/03) [2005] 2 CMLR 27

Nicknames Cases are often referred to by nicknames. For example, Case 120/78 *Rewe-Zentral AG* v *Bundesmonopolverwaltung für Branntwein* [1979] ECR 649 is often referred to as *"Cassis de Dijon"*. When searching, try to use the party names, case number or ECR reference. If you do not know this, you can search secondary sources using the nickname to find the formal reference given in footnotes.

Aids to finding ECJ case law

The most useful sources for finding case law from the ECJ and CFI are the search and browse functions on online services. These allow you to search by case number or reference, party names and subject.

- *"Curia"*: basic search and advanced search have lots of options including party names, dates and subject keywords.
- *Westlaw*: the "EU" search screen has "Case or Document No", "Parties or Title" and "Free text" fields.
- *Lexis®Library*: the "International Cases" search screen provides "Citation", "Case name", and "Search terms" fields.
- *Lawtel*: the "EU Cases" search screen provides "Case Number", "Case Name", "Summary", and "Keywords" fields.
- *Justis EU*: the search screen provides fields including "Title", "Reference", "Full Text" and "Subject".

- *EUR-Lex*: in addition to other options, the "Simple Search" provides the option to search by *European Court Reports* publication reference. You can also browse the *Directory of European Union case Law*.

Print sources which are useful for locating ECJ case law include:

- *European Current Law*: the *Year Book* may be browsed by subject heading or its index and "Cumulative List of Cases" used to locate cases by subject or name.
- *Official Journal*: the alphabetical index and methodological table give references in the "C" series.
- *Encyclopaedias and textbooks:* indexes and tables of cases provide references to cases.

INTERNATIONAL LAW

Public international law

Public international law is the body of law which governs relationships between states, international organisations, and occasionally individuals. It covers a wide and diverse range of subject areas which include maritime law, the laws of armed conflict, international trade law, and human rights law amongst others. It is important to distinguish public international law from private international law which aims to regulate private relationships across national borders.

There are two international courts: the International Court of Justice and the International Criminal Court. The Court of Justice is the primary judicial organ of the United Nations and deals primarily with civil disputes between states. The Criminal Court deals with serious criminal cases involving, for example, genocide, war crimes, and crimes against humanity. It only has jurisdiction over those states (and nationals of those states) who agreed to the creation of the Criminal Court.

European human rights law

Human rights law, as a branch of international law, has become increasingly important in the UK. The European Convention on Human Rights and Fundamental Freedoms (ECHR) is a treaty drafted by the Council of Europe (a treaty organisation entirely distinct from the European Union). The European Court of Human Rights was established to ensure that states comply with their obligations under the Convention.

The Scotland Act 1998 and the Human Rights Act 1998 both incorporated the ECHR into the domestic law of the UK. This effectively means that the jurisprudence of the European Court of Human Rights must be applied by UK courts.

Sources of international law

Treaties

A treaty is a written international agreement between states (or some international organisations). Treaties may also be termed "conventions", "agreements", "charters", "declarations" or "protocols". A treaty agreed between two states is "bilateral". A treaty agreed between more than two states is "multilateral".

The individual provisions comprising a treaty are usually known as articles and paragraphs. A treaty is binding only on those states who have signed and ratified it and then only once it has come into force.

In some states, such as the UK, a treaty requires implementation by domestic legislation to be binding in domestic law.

Case law

International courts and tribunals exist to apply and interpret treaties and other rules of international law. The International Court of Justice decides legal disputes between states and offers advisory opinions to the United Nations and other authorised agencies. However, a system of precedent does not operate in the same way as in Scottish courts.

Other international courts of special jurisdiction exist, for example: the International Criminal Court, the Central American Court of Justice, WTO Dispute Settlement Body Panels, and the European Court of Human Rights.

Custom

Customary international law evolves from the practice of states over time. For a custom to be accepted there must be recognition by states that the practice amounts to a binding obligation in international law. Custom may be established in case law or may be codified in treaties.

Travaux préparatoires/conference proceedings

These materials, preparatory to final treaties, are not legally binding themselves but may be referred to when interpreting the meaning of a treaty.

Model laws

Model laws may be drafted by international organisations to provide guidance to states when creating domestic law. For example, UNIDROIT has adopted model laws on leasing and franchise disclosure as well as "Principles of International Commercial Contracts". Model laws are not binding on states but may be adopted domestically or used as guidance when interpreting national law.

Where to find sources of international law

Treaties

Treaties may be found in a number of printed collections, some of which are reproduced online.

United Kingdom Treaty Series (1892–) This series is published by the Foreign and Commonwealth Office (FCO). It contains treaties ratified by the UK. The FCO has now made a database of UK treaties available online. You can link to it from the GOV.UK UK treaties page (https://www.gov.uk/guidance/uk-treaties), which has lots of useful information about procedures as well as links to the full text of treaty documents. As treaties in this series are published as Command Papers they are also available from online subscription services including *House of Commons Parliamentary Papers* and *Public Information Online* (see Chapter 3 for more information about these services).

Treaties subject to ratification, or a similar procedure, are laid before the UK Parliament and published as Command Papers as part of the FCO's "Country Series" (bilateral), "Miscellaneous Series" (multilateral), or "European Community Series". Once ratified, they are republished in the "Treaty Series".

United Nations Treaty Series (UNTS) (1946–) This important modern collection contains treaties registered with, and published by, the UN Secretariat. It includes treaties to which the UK is not party.

A searchable database for the UNTS is available via the *UN Treaty Collection* site (http://treaties.un.org). This database provides links, where possible, to full-text treaties.

The *League of Nations Treaty Series* (1920–1946) and the *Consolidated Treaty Series* (covering 1628–1919) provide sources of treaties pre-dating the UN.

International Legal Materials (1962–) Published by the American Society of International Law, ILM reproduces the full text of important treaties as well as other international law documents. ILM is available online on *Lexis®Library* (1962–), *Westlaw International* (selected coverage 1980–) and *HeinOnline* (1962–).

The text of treaties and other primary materials are reproduced in textbooks and other secondary sources. For example, I Brownlie, *Basic Documents in International Law* (6th edn, 2008) collects together key treaties and other documents relevant to the study of international law. International materials may also be included in "cases and materials" books or student statute collections on specific areas of law.

Case law

A number of series of law reports containing decisions of international courts and tribunals. The more significant series include:

Reports of Judgments, Advisory Opinions and Orders of the International Court of Justice This is the official series of International Court of Justice decisions from 1947 onwards. A list of all cases before the court since 1947 is available via http://www.icj-cij.org (under "Cases"). Where available, links are given to the full text of judgments and opinions.

International Law Reports This series contains decisions of international courts, tribunals and arbitrators as well as national courts. The series covers the period from 1919 onwards. Before 1950 the series was called the *Annual Digest and Reports of Public International Law Cases*. *International Law Reports* is available on *Justis*.

International Legal Materials In addition to reproducing other international materials, ILM contains the text of important judicial decisions. ILM is available online on *Lexis®Library* (1962–), *Westlaw International* (selected coverage 1980–) and *HeinOnline* (1962–).

Reports of Judgments and Decisions: European Court of Human Rights This is the official series of decisions of the court. The series was preceded by *European Court of Human Rights: Series A: Judgments and Decisions* (1961–1996).

The case law of the European Court of Human Rights is available online on the public access *HUDOC* database (http://www.echr.coe.int/ ECHR/EN/hudoc).

Custom

By its very nature, customary international law is difficult to locate in documents. Textbooks on international law may indicate customs accepted as creating binding obligations on states.

Model laws

Model laws may be published in print by the organisations adopting them and may also appear on their websites. Model laws may also be reproduced in secondary materials.

Travaux préparatoires

Given that many treaties are negotiated behind closed doors, *travaux préparatoires* may prove difficult to locate. The preparatory work which is available may be published in print by the organisation which drafted the treaty or by an independent publisher (often as "conference proceedings"). Alternatively, *travaux préparatoires* may appear on the website of the relevant international organisation. For example, *travaux préparatoires* for the ECHR are available from the European Court of Human Rights site (http://www.echr.coe.int/Library/).

Online sources

Sources of international law are available from a number of online services.

WordLII (http://www.worldlii.org/) A key freely accessible website is the *World Legal Information Institute* (part of the Free Access to Law movement). *WorldLII* provides access to many international decisions and treaties.

Eagle-i Internet **Portal for Law** (http://ials.sas.ac.uk/eaglei/project/ eiproject.htm) provides links to freely available quality legal sites and sources including international law. Search or browse by country, resource type or keyword.

EISIL (http://www.eisil.org/) The *Electronic Information System for International Law* has been developed by the American Society for International Law. *EISIL* provides information about, and access to, international law materials and includes a browsable directory and a searchable database.

Subscription services   Online subscription database services provide access to a range of full-text international materials. What you have access to will depend on your library's subscriptions. *Westlaw International* can be accessed from the *Westlaw UK* homepage under "Services" and on *Lexis®Library* international material can be accessed under the "Sources" tab.

How to find sources of international law

Aids to finding international law

Treaties   Tools to help you locate treaties by title, date, subject and party include:

- Printed indexes. For example: the annual *Index to Treaty Series* (part of the *UK Treaty Series*, published as a Command Paper), indexes to the *United Nations Treaty Series*, the *International Law Reports* consolidated table of treaties, and *International Legal Materials* annual subject indexes and cumulative indexes (also available on *Westlaw International*).
- Search and browse functions on the *FCO, UN Treaty Collection* and *EISIL* websites, and on subscription databases providing access to treaty series.
- *FLARE Index to Treaties* (http://ials.sas.ac.uk/library/flag/introtreaties. htm) – a database of information on significant multilateral treaties from 1856 onwards. The database provides details of where to find the full text of treaties in print and online.

Cases   Tools to help you locate cases include:
- Printed and online indexes. For example, the annual index to *Reports of Judgments, Advisory Opinions and Orders of the International Court of Justice* are published in print and are made available online (http:// www.un.org/law/ICJsummaries/), the consolidated index to the *International Law Reports* (available online at http://www.lcil.cam. ac.uk/publications/international-law-reports) and *International Legal Materials* annual subject and cumulative indexes (also available on *Westlaw International*).
- Search and browse functions on public access and subscription database services providing access to international case law.

Citation

Treaties A treaty is usually cited by title and date of signature (and place of signature, if multilateral), for example:

> Marrakesh Agreement establishing the World Trade Organization, 15 April 1994

(**NB** This might be referred to by a colloquial title, eg "WTO Agreement" or "Marrakesh Agreement".)

The citation might also include a reference to one or more of the series in which the treaty is published:

> Marrakesh Agreement establishing the World Trade Organization, 15 April 1994, 1867 UNTS 154, 33 ILM 1114

Common citations include:

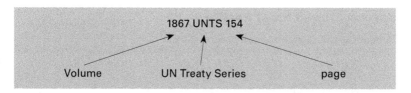

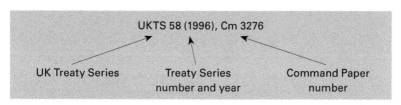

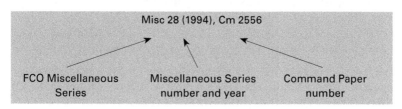

Cases If reported, the case may be referred to by case name and report, for example:

> *Case Concerning Legality of Use of Force (Serbia and Montenegro* v *Belgium)* 2004 ICJ Rep 128
>
> *Application of the Convention on the Prevention and Punishment of Genocide (Bosnia-Herzegovina* v *Serbia),* Judgment of 26 Feb 2007, (2007) 46 ILM 188

Cases not formally reported may be referred to by a court reference number and judgment date. For example, a case from the International Criminal Tribunal for Rwanda may be cited as:

> *Prosecutor* v *Akayesu* (Case No ICTR-96-4-T) Judgment of 2 September 1998

Checking the status of treaties

When using a treaty you may need to check:

- who are the parties to it;
- whether it is in force; and
- whether a party has ratified it.

Of particular use in finding information about the status of a multilateral treaty are the *Multilateral Treaties Deposited with the Secretary-General (MTDSG)* and *UN Treaty Series (UNTS)* databases, both available from the *UN Treaty Collection* website (http://treaties.un.org). *UNTS* and *MTDSG* records include details of parties ("participants"), actions (ratification, acceptance, accession, etc), and entry into force (EIF).

For treaties to which the UK is a signatory, information about status may be obtained from the FCO's Treaty Enquiry Service (see http://www.fco.gov.uk/en/about-us/publications-and-documents/treaties/enquiries-service) or by checking on the UK Treaties Online (UKTO) database http://treaties.fco.gov.uk/treaties/treaty.htm

FOREIGN LAW

Sources of foreign law

In many countries primary sources of law may be categorised in a similar way to those of UK jurisdictions, ie legislation and case law.

Legislation from other countries may be revoked or amended and judicially interpreted. In common law jurisdictions (eg USA, Canada, or Australia) systems of precedent operate in relation to case law. Some countries contain more than one jurisdiction – for example, in the USA individual states have their own legislatures and courts but federal laws apply across all states.

Secondary sources such as books and journals are also produced for non-UK jurisdictions, and the governments and legislatures of other countries produce their own official publications.

Where to find sources of foreign law

It is not possible here to cover the wide variety of foreign legal systems and their sources of legal information. However, some useful sources for beginning research on a foreign jurisdiction are highlighted.

Websites

Many websites offer access to foreign legal materials. A useful general legal internet gateway is the *Eagle-i Internet Portal for Law*, which provides access to material from many jurisdictions.

Eagle-i Internet Portal for Law (http://ials.sas.ac.uk/eaglei/project/eiproject.htm) provides guidance on, and access to, online legal information resources from around the world. Subject specialists select and evaluate sites which provide access to primary and secondary legal materials. Use the "Filter by country" drop-down to select other jurisductions.

Online subscription services

With the appropriate subscriptions, several subscription services provide access to material from non-UK jurisdictions.

Westlaw International *Westlaw International* can be accessed from the Westlaw UK homepage under "Services". Content includes:

- United States: federal and state legislation and case law, journals/law reviews and other secondary materials.
- Canada: federal and provincial legislation and case law, journals/law reviews and other secondary materials.
- Australia: federal and state/territory case law, journals, and other secondary materials.

Lexis®Library Non-UK material can be accessed under the "Sources" tab. Content includes:

- United States: federal and state legislation and case law, journals/law reviews and other secondary materials.
- Canada: federal and provincial legislation and case law, journals/law reviews and other secondary materials.
- Australia: federal and state/territory case law and journals.
- New Zealand: case law and commentary.
- South Africa: case law and legislation.

Print sources

Your library may hold sources of foreign legal information and other libraries to which you have access may hold relevant collections. You can use individual institution catalogues online or union library catalogues (eg COPAC http://copac.jisc.ac.uk/) to locate material or use *FLAG*.

FLAG (http://ials.sas.ac.uk/library/flag/flag.htm)   *FLAG* (Foreign Law Guide) is a gateway providing information about holdings of foreign, international and comparative law in UK universities and national libraries. *FLAG* can be searched by jurisdiction, form of material (legislation, law reports, digests, etc), and subject.

By using either the "Search the collections" or "Advanced search" options you can retrieve information about which libraries hold collections relating to particular jurisdictions.

Essential Facts

European Union law

- The primary sources of EU law are legislation and case law.
- Legislation includes: primary legislation – Treaties establishing the EU; and secondary legislation – Regulations, Directives, Decisions. Directives require implementation through national legislation.
- EU legislation and case law can be found in official print sources: *Official Journal* "L" Series and *European Court Reports*.
- EU legislation and case law can also be found online using public access services (*EUR-Lex* and "*Curia*") and subscription services.

International and foreign law

- Primary sources of international law include treaties, case law and custom.

- Human rights law is an important branch of international law. The European Convention on Human Rights has been imported into Scots law through the Scotland Act 1998 and the Human Rights Act 1998.

- Treaties may be published in one or more treaty series and cases reported in one or more series of reports.

- When using a treaty you may need to check who the parties are, whether they have ratified the treaty, and whether it has come into force.

- Sources of foreign legal information may fall into the same broad categories as sources of Scots and UK law.

- Online access to sources of foreign and international law is available from a number of subscription and public access services. *Intute: Law* is a gateway providing access to material from many jurisdictions.

Further Reading

- S Switzer, *European Law Essentials* (2009).
- I Brownlie, *Principles of Public International Law* (8th edn, 2012).
- F Grant, *Legal Research Skills for Scots Lawyers* (3rd edn, 2014), Chapters 10 and 11.
- J Knowles, *Effective Legal Research* (4th edn, 2016), Chapter 8.
- P A Thomas and J Knowles, *Dane and Thomas' How to Use a Law Library* (4th edn, 2001), Chapter 12.

9 BOOKS, JOURNALS AND OTHER SOURCES

Here we consider various types of secondary source, what they are most useful for, how to use them and how to find them. We also look at other important sources including institutional writings and reports of the Law Commissions.

Books and journals, as secondary sources of legal information, offer commentary on the law. They can point you towards authoritative primary sources and provide an overall picture of the law in a particular area.

An up-to-date legal textbook is often the best starting point for legal research and is a good way of getting a grounding in the law in a particular area and of identifying relevant authorities that you can follow up. Journal articles too are an excellent source for understanding the law in a particular area and offer argument and debate which help inform your own opinions. Secondary sources are an essential part of your legal research and you should develop skills in handling them and using them to your best advantage in just the same way as you do for specialist primary sources and tools.

INSTITUTIONAL WRITERS

Institutional writings, also known as authoritative writings, are the works of writers who first brought together the principles of Scots law into legal texts. These institutional writers lived mostly during the 17th and 18th centuries but their work has proved to be highly influential in the development of Scots law. Although their influence has dwindled somewhat in modern times, a statement made by an institutional writer will settle the law if there is no statute or judicial precedent covering the area in question. These works are considered a minor formal, or primary, source of Scots law.

Some of the most important institutional writers are as follows:

- Sir Thomas Craig, *Jus Feudal* (1655, trans 1934);
- James Dalrymple, Viscount Stair, *The Institutions of the Law of Scotland* (1681, 6th edn 1981);
- Andrew McDouall, Lord Bankton, *An Institute of the Laws of Scotland* (1751–53);
- John Erskine, *An Institute of the Law of Scotland* (1773, 8th edn 1871);

- George Joseph Bell, *Commentaries on the Laws of Scotland and Principles of Mercantile Jurisprudence* (1804, 7th edn 1870) and *Principles of the Law of Scotland* (1829, 10th edn 1899);
- Archibald Alison, *Principles of the Criminal Law of Scotland* (1832) and *Practice of the Criminal Law of Scotland* (1833);
- David Hume, *Commentaries on the Law of Scotland, Respecting the Description and Punishment of Crimes* (1797, 4th edn 1844);
- Sir George MacKenzie, *The Laws and Customs of Scotland in Matters Criminal* (1678, 2nd edn 1699).

Structure and citation

Institutional works are not all arranged in the same way. A work may be comprised of several "books" divided into "chapters" or "titles"; in turn, these may be subdivided into sections or paragraphs. Furthermore, a work may consist of several volumes – each volume may contain more than one "book".

It is common to see citations to institutional works in abbreviated form, eg:

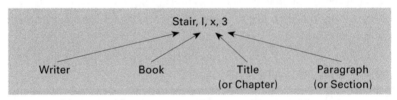

This citation is a reference to Book I, Title X, paragraph 3 of Stair's *Institutions*.

LAW COMMISSION REPORTS AND CONSULTATION PAPERS

The Scottish Law Commission and the Law Commission of England and Wales are statutory bodies created to review the law and recommend reform where appropriate. As part of the process they issue consultations and reports.

Law Commission Reports

Many reports of the Law Commission of England and Wales are published as Command Papers or House of Commons Papers. Scottish Law Commission Reports may now be published as SG Papers (formerly SE Papers) or House of Commons Papers; prior to the creation of the Scottish Parliament in 1999 they may have been published as Command Papers (see Chapter 3).

Where to find Law Commission Reports

The Law Commissions' Reports are available in collections of Command Papers, HC Papers and SG papers on *HCPP* and *Public Information Online* (see Chapter 3). In addition, they are also freely available from the Law Commission websites:

- *Law Commission (of England and Wales)* (http://www.lawcom.gov.uk/) – Reports from 1995 onwards are available;
- *Scottish Law Commission* (http://www.scotlawcom.gov.uk/) – Reports from 1965 onwards are available.

Libraries may hold separate collections of the Law Commissions' reports arranged by report number.

Citation

In addition to a Command Paper, HC Paper or SG Paper number, reports are assigned a "Law Com" or "Scot Law Com" report number:

> Scottish Law Commission, *Report on Succession* (Scot Law Com No 215, SG/2009/45, 2009)
>
> Law Commission, *Intoxication and Criminal Liability* (Law Com No 314, Cm 7526, 2009)

Finding a report

- *Public Information Online* and *HCPP* (subscription databases) allow you to search for papers by title or by paper number.
- The Commissions' websites provide free access to reports. Search by title/ keyword or area of law on the Law Commission website. Reports are listed in date and number order on the Scottish Law Commission website as well as in a summary table (these are all hyperlinked to the full report).
- If you need to find full details of any Commission publications, the *UKOP* database facilitates searching by title, keyword, issuing body, date, etc. Records provide full publication details including Command Paper, HC Paper, Law Com/Scot Law Com, and SG Paper numbers.

Law Commission Discussion/Consultation Papers

Where to find Discussion/Consultation Papers

The Commissions' websites provide access to discussion and consultation papers online. Some libraries hold collections of Scottish Law Commission Discussion Papers and Law Commission Consultation Papers, which will be listed in catalogues (searchable online) with holdings and location information.

Citation

Discussion/consultation papers may be cited as:

> Scottish Law Commission, *Discussion Paper on Succession* (Scot Law Com DP No 136, 2007)
>
> Law Commission, *Consultation Paper on Intoxication and Criminal Liability* (Law Com CP 127, 1993)

OTHER OFFICIAL PUBLICATIONS

Parliamentary publications are considered fully in Chapter 3. Government departments, agencies, and other public bodies produce many other "non-parliamentary" official publications. These may be published as books and journals and be found in libraries in the same way as other books and journals. However, a large number of official publications are now available online from the websites of relevant organisations. Useful tools for locating official publications online include:

GOV.UK (http://www.gov.uk/)   Provides links to the sites of ministerial departments, other (non-ministerial) government departments and agencies/public bodies. Individual sites contain links to departmental and agency publications. There is also a site-wide publications search which searches across all publications. (The "Publications" link is at the bottom of the screen.)

Scottish   Government   (http://www.scotland.gov.uk/sol.)   The "Publications" link provides access to many departmental and agency publications.

UKOP   This subscription database allows you to search by title, keyword, issuing body, date, etc to find full publication details. Links are provided to full text documents online (where available).

BOOKS

Textbooks

A textbook contains an author's statement of, and commentary on, the law. There are different types of textbooks – aimed at different audiences – which you can use for different purposes. These include:

- student texts, which provide a basic introduction to an area of law;
- cases and materials books, which collect together key cases, legislation, and commentary in a single work;
- practitioner texts, which provide detailed treatment of an area of law and are used as "reference works"; and
- monographs, which consider a specific topic in detail.

There is overlap between these categories – especially in a small jurisdiction such as Scotland.

While not having the status of institutional works, some textbooks are treated as providing an authoritative statement of the law. For example, Sir William Wade's seminal text *Administrative Law* (11th edn, 2014), published by the Oxford University Press, and titles published under the auspices of the Scottish Universities Law Institute (SULI) are particularly well regarded.

Editions and supplements

The law is constantly evolving and textbooks reflect this in being produced in new, updated, editions regularly. As a rule of thumb, you should use the most recent edition of a textbook available to you and be conscious of the date it was published and when you are reading it.

Supplements are produced for some textbooks which "bridge the gap" between editions and highlight changes in the law since the main work. If a supplement exists, it should be read together with the textbook to give a more up-to-date picture of the law.

Using textbooks

As a student, it is unlikely that you will read a textbook from beginning to end. You are more likely to be referred to specific chapters or pages by your lecturer. How you use it will depend on what you need to know. There are features of legal textbooks you should be aware of and which can help you make most effective use of them:

- Currency – given the time between the writing and publication of a book, the preface of legal textbooks will often state the date at which the law can be taken to be accurate. This is so that you, the reader, can check for changes in the law subsequent to that date (eg by checking the status of cases and legislation referred to in the text).
- Table of contents – use this to focus your reading on chapters (or parts of chapters) of most relevance to you. Legal textbooks are often structured like reference works and allow for "dipping in".

- Tables of cases and legislation – these list cases and legislation referred to in the book with page references.
- Footnotes/endnotes – give references or may explain in more detail a point in the main work. These are a valuable pointer to further resources for research and should be used fully.
- Index – lists topics covered in the book alphabetically with page references. The index is normally more detailed than the contents pages and might be worth browsing in addition to the table of contents.

You should also be aware of the jurisdiction the book covers. While many textbooks covering UK or English law may take account of areas where Scots law differs, some may not.

Encyclopaedias

A legal encyclopaedia is a work which aims to give a comprehensive statement of the law. Some, like the *Scottish Planning Encyclopaedia*, cover a specific area of law, while others, such as *The Laws of Scotland: Stair Memorial Encyclopaedia*, are much broader in scope.

The Laws of Scotland: Stair Memorial Encyclopaedia

Often referred to simply as the *Stair Memorial Encyclopaedia*, this work provides an updated narrative statement of Scots law. It is a very useful starting point for legal research, especially on a topic of which you have no prior knowledge. It is available online and in print.

The work comprises 130 "titles" (general subjects) from "Administrative Law" to "Wills and Succession". Within each "title" the subject is divided into more specific headings, subheadings, and numbered paragraphs.

Online *The Laws of Scotland* is available via the subscription database *Lexis®Library* (listed under "Commentary").

You can search or browse the encyclopaedia. Searching across the entire work means that you will retrieve documents matching your search terms, whichever title they appear under. You may find it easier to browse the work and then select particular titles or headings to search under – this limits results to those particular topics.

Each numbered paragraph is comprised of the original text and update text. The updating text appears as separate "TEXT" and "NOTE" entries below the original text and footnotes. Updates are not incorporated into the main text – you must read the whole paragraph.

Print *The Laws of Scotland* was originally published in 25 volumes, titles appeared alphabetically within these volumes. To reflect changes in the law, a number of titles have been updated and reissued as individual booklets. These booklets are held in "Reissue" binders and supersede the title in the original volume. Each volume and reissue booklet contains a table of contents and an index. Because original volumes are retained on the shelf until all titles have been reissued, you must always check whether a reissue exists and, if so, use that rather than the original text. Reissues and original volumes are updated by the annual *Cumulative Supplement* and this is updated during each year by the *Noter-up* in the *Service Binder*.

The *Consolidated Index*, *Consolidated Table of Cases*, and *Consolidated Table of Statutes etc* are each issued annually and refer you to topics, cases, and legislative provisions in the encyclopaedia. References are to volume or reissue and paragraph number.

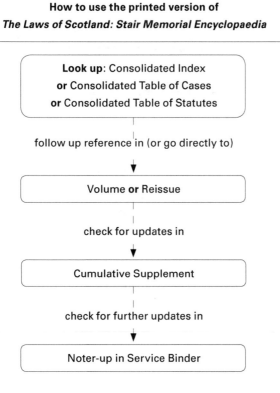

Halsbury's Laws of England

Halsbury's Laws of England is a comprehensive encyclopaedia of English law. It is the English equivalent of the *Stair Memorial Encyclopaedia* and is highly regarded. It is a key resource for researching UK-wide or English law. It is now into its fifth edition and comprises a number of "titles" (or subjects). It is available in print and online via the subscription database *Lexis®Library*.

Online The online version is accessed and used in a similar way to the online version of *The Laws of Scotland*. It is listed as "Halsbury's Laws of England" under "Commentary" on *Lexis®Library*.

Print The print version comprises a large number of volumes which are updated and reissued to reflect changes in the law. Each volume contains a table of contents and an index. *Cumulative Supplement* volumes are issued annually and indicate changes in the law since the bound volumes' publication and the *Current Service*, comprised of the *Monthly Review* and *Noter-up*, gives information on changes since the last *Cumulative Supplement*.

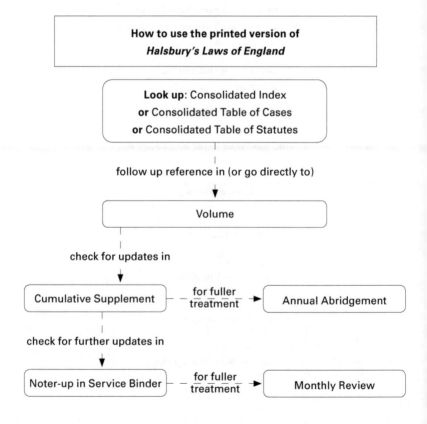

The *Consolidated Index* and *Consolidated Tables* of statutes and cases volumes are issued annually. References are to volume and paragraph number.

Annual Abridgements consolidate each year's monthly reviews and contain summaries of cases and legislation.

Looseleaf encyclopaedic works

A number of texts give a comprehensive account of specific areas of law. These collect together revised versions of statutes, summaries of cases and commentary together in a single work. Many of these are now published as "looseleaf" works. These consist of binders, which allow pages to be removed and new pages to be inserted. Texts can be updated to take account of changes in the law.

When using a looseleaf work, you should check the date at which the last update was filed and the date at which the work claims to accurately state the law. You can locate relevant material within the work by using the index and tables of cases and legislation. References are usually to paragraphs within the work. Some looseleafs may be comprised of several volumes.

Useful Scottish looseleaf works include:

- *Parliament House Book* – contains legislation relating to Scottish private law and court procedure;
- *Renton and Brown's Criminal Procedure According to the Law of Scotland* and *Criminal Procedure Legislation* (both also available on *Westlaw*); and
- *McEwan and Paton on Damages for Personal Injury in Scotland.*

Styles and precedents collections

A "style" (or in England a "precedent") is a template for a legal document (eg a contract, writ, or will) which can be adapted by the practitioner. Notable Scottish collections include:

- *Green's Practice Styles*;
- *Green's Litigation Styles*;
- S Bennett, *Style Writs for the Sheriff Court* (4th edn, 2009).

The Encyclopaedia of Forms and Precedents is a multiple volume work which is regularly updated. While published for a largely English audience, it is of use to the Scottish practitioner. It is also available via the subscription database *Lexis®Library*.

Legal dictionaries

There are two broad categories of legal dictionary – the "glossary" and the "judicial dictionary".

Glossaries

Glossaries explain the meaning of legal terms, including Latin words and phrases. Modern examples include:

- J E Penner (ed), *The Law Student's Dictionary* (13th edn, 2008)
- M Woodley (ed), *Osborn's Concise Law Dictionary* (12th edn, 2013)

Of particular relevance to Scots law are:

- G Watson, *Bell's Dictionary and Digest of the Law of Scotland* (7th edn, 1890);
- S R O'Rourke, *Glossary of Legal Terms* (6th edn, 2014);
- W J Stewart, *Collin's Dictionary of Law* (3rd edn, 2006) – edited by a Scottish lawyer;
- S Styles and N R Whitty, *Glossary: Scottish and European Union Legal Terms and Latin Phrases* (2nd edn, 2003);
- J Trayner, *Trayner's Latin Maxims* (4th edn, 1894, reprinted 1998).

Judicial dictionaries

Judicial dictionaries give the meaning of words as defined in legislation and interpreted by judges and give references to relevant cases and statutes. Examples include:

- D Greenberg, *Stroud's Judicial Dictionary of Words and Phrases* (8th edn, 2012; supplements are published annually);
- D Hay (ed), *Words and Phrases Legally Defined* (4th edn, 2007; supplements are published annually).

Of particular relevance to Scots law are:

- A W Dalrymple and A D Gibb, *Scottish Judicial Dictionary: Dictionary of Words and Phrases: Judicially Defined and commented on by the Scottish Supreme Courts* (1946);
- W J Stewart, *Scottish Contemporary Judicial Dictionary of Words and Phrases* (1995) – covers period 1946–1993.

Directories

Legal directories list contact details for law firms, solicitors, and other legal organisations. *The Scottish Law Directory: The White Book* is published annually with the authority of the Law Society of Scotland. It includes lists of certificated solicitors and Scottish law firms.

An online searchable directory of Scottish solicitors is available from the Law Society of Scotland website (http://www.lawscot.org.uk/) by following the link "Find a Solicitor".

An online directory of members of the Faculty of Advocates is available from the Faculty's website at: http://www.advocates.org.uk/.

Where to find books

Print sources

You will find print books in the library either for loan or as reference items. Textbooks are likely to be available as multiple copies and for loan. Updating (looseleaf) works and multi-volume works are more likely to be for reference only.

Online.

Increasingly, legal textbooks are available online and will be accessible via the library catalogue. Some titles are available through database services (eg *Westlaw*, *Lexis®Library* and *HeinOnline*).

How to find books

Sources which will help you find books include: course notes, library catalogues, footnotes and bibliographies, legal bibliographies, and publishers' and booksellers' websites. You may need to find:

- a specific book to which you have found a reference; or
- books on a topic you are researching.

Citation

A full reference to a textbook is given in the form:

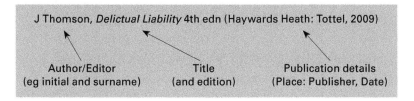

J Thomson, *Delictual Liability* 4th edn (Haywards Heath: Tottel, 2009)

| Author/Editor (eg initial and surname) | Title (and edition) | Publication details (Place: Publisher, Date) |

NB Author information may be given in the form Surname, Forename (eg Thomson, Joe) and there may be more than one author.

If a reference is to an essay or chapter within a book then the reference is given in the form:

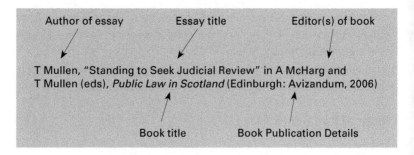

Author of essay   Essay title   Editor(s) of book

T Mullen, "Standing to Seek Judicial Review" in A McHarg and
T Mullen (eds), *Public Law in Scotland* (Edinburgh: Avizandum, 2006)

Book title   Book Publication Details

NB When following up this type of reference you should search catalogues using the name of the *editor* and *title of the book* (*not* the essay author and title, which is a common mistake).

Library catalogues

Library catalogues provided an index of all holdings and you can ussually sarch by:

- author/editor;
- title;
- keywords.

How you search will depend on what information you have.

Title search Title search is the most direct search if you are working from a reading list or reference.

Keyword search Use this to find books on a particular topic. This search will normally match your search terms against the book record, which might include the book summary and table of contents, but it does not search the whole book. This means that you need to consider the most appropriate search terms (and may need to use broad headings).

Search results Results will list all books matching your search terms and will normally include the print book and the ebook, if this is available. Book records will include bibliographic details (author, title, edition, date of publication) and often enhanced information like a summary, the table of contents and sometimes book reviews. You will also find details of where the book is shelved (relevant level/floor of the library and the shelf number).

If you cannot find a book in your own library, you can check the catalogues of other libraries. Library catalogues are usually accessible online on the institution website. COPAC (http://copac.jisc.ac.uk/) is a union catalogue of UK and Irish academic, national and specialist libraries and is a good way of finding out where books are held or where there are good collections.

SCONUL Access (http://www.sconul.ac.uk/sconul-access) is a free reciprocal borrowing scheme in the UK which facilitates reference access and borrowing rights for staff and students of participating HE institutions. So if there are libraries with rich print collections in your research area, you may want to use the SCONUL Access scheme to get access or borrowing rights for that library. Full terms of the scheme are available on the website.

If you do not have borrowing rights at another library, you can also use the inter-library loan service of your own library to get material from elsewhere.

Other ways to find books

Footnotes and bibliographies References within textbooks and journal articles are a great way of finding other relevant textbooks. Footnotes appear at the bottom of a page where a reference is made in the text. Endnotes group together references at the end of a chapter or article. Bibliographies list all texts used in the preparation of a book or article and provide an "at-a-glance" list of further reading on a topic. If you are reading a particularly good book, it is always worth following up on footnotes and endnotes. Well-researched books are a great source of related material.

Legal bibliographies These list law books under subject headings:

- *Current Law Year Books* contain details of books published in each year under subject headings and in a list of books at the back of the final volume. Information for the current year is given month by month in the *Monthly Digest*.

Publishers' and booksellers' websites The sites of individual publishers (eg Edinburgh University Press – http://www.edinburghuniversitypress. com/) and booksellers have online searchable catalogues of published books. Notable legal booksellers include:

- Avizandum Law Bookshop (http://www.avizandum.co.uk/);
- Hammicks Legal Information Services (http://www.hammickslegal. com/live/);
- Wildy & Sons Ltd (http://www.wildy.com).

JOURNALS

Journals are a key source for any academic research as they are published widely in academia and provide discussion and debate. They are also usually well referenced and as they are such an important part of academic literature, they are cited and referenced by other articles and so are a rich source of information.

Journals are published in parts, or issues, throughout the year and at the end of a year these parts may be bound into a single volume. However, it is much more likely that you will encounter journal articles online as the move from print to digital for journals happened very quickly and most subscriptions now are to the online version. There are still collections of print journals in libraries but retrospective digitisation means that even older material is available online.

Within each journal part there are articles on different topics by different authors. Some legal journals contain news items or summaries of cases as well. Like books, different journals are aimed at different audiences:

- Practitioner journals (written by legal practitioners for their peers) are published frequently and contain current awareness articles. Examples include the *Journal of the Law Society of Scotland* and the *Solicitors' Journal*.
- Academic journals contain well-researched scholarly articles often on theoretical issues. Examples include *Juridical Review*, *Edinburgh Law Review* and *Modern Law Review*.

Journals may cover legal topics in general or may have a specialist focus (eg *Construction Law Journal*). They may cover Scottish, UK or European jurisdictions and there are also many foreign legal journals.

In Scotland, of particular note is *Scots Law Times* (SLT). While categorised as a series of law reports, SLT contains a "News" section with articles and news items.

Where to find journals

Print sources

Law libraries usually hold a number of journal titles in print. These will tend to be older journal collections but the catalogue will confirm the coverage dates.

Often they are held in a distinct section (separate from law reports) and may be separated by jurisdiction. Journals may be arranged alphabetically by title or may be arranged according to classification. The current year's issues may be displayed in a separate section.

Online

There are many ways to find and access legal journals online. Some are available freely on websites such as *EJLT* (*European Journal of Law and Technology* at http://ejlt.org/index) but most are only available through subscription services.

Academic libraries tend to buy journals in packages (called "big deals") which means that they provide access to thousands of journal titles (millions of articles) from the major journal publishers. These deals are normally negotiated at a national level and in Scotland this is done via the SHEDL (Scottish Higher Education Digital Library) consortium. This means that most academic institutions in Scotland have access to the same current journal packages from the large publishers.

As well as providing access to journals directly from the publisher, libraries provide access via subscriptions to online databases. Databases are usually a mix of full text and bibliographic references (ie information about published articles, including an abstract):

- *Westlaw* provides access to full-text articles from many UK journals via its "Journals" search screen. (This search also provides *Legal Journals Index* abstracts (summaries) of many more articles not available in full text on *Westlaw UK*.)

- *Lexis®Library* also provides access to full-text articles from UK journals via its "Journals" search. (This search also provides abstracts of articles not available in full text on *Lexis®Library*. These are from *Lexis®Library*'s "UK Journals Index".)

- *HeinOnline* provides access to full-text PDF versions of articles from predominantly US journals via its "Law Journal Library".

There is little overlap in UK journal coverage between these services – so you should check all services to which you have access when trying to locate a particular journal. With the relevant subscription, *Westlaw* and *Lexis®Library* also provide access to a range of US and other foreign journals. These may be accessed under "Westlaw International", or the "Sources" tab on *Lexis®Library*.

How to find journal articles

Aids to finding articles

Since academic journals are principally available online, and there are so many online services, it is possible to find journal articles via a number of different routes. Traditionally print indexes were created which allowed the researcher to locate journal literature using subject headings, authors, publication title, etc. These moved online as abstracting and indexing databases and have gradually developed to include some full text articles. One such index is the *Legal Journals Index*, which is now available online via *Westlaw*. *LJI* covers the period from 1986 and provides details and abstracts of substantive articles from over 800 journals. It is the most comprehensive index of UK legal journals.

Lexis®Library contains its own "UK Journals Index", *Lawtel UK* contains an "Articles Index", and *JustCite* provides an "Articles" search. These services provide abstracts of articles, including information about where the article was published.

Abstracts on *Westlaw* or *Lexis®Library* provide a link to the full-text article if it is also available on those services. A *JustCite* abstract provides links to available sources of the full-text article.

Abstracts give details of:

- the title and author of the article;
- a short content summary; and
- details of the journal in which the article was published.

Current Law The *Monthly Digest* provides summaries of journal articles month by month throughout the year.

Online databases A number of online subscription databases for social science and humanities are useful for finding legal journal articles. Examples include:

- *Applied Social Sciences Index and Abstracts* (ASSIA);
- *British Humanities Index*;
- *International Bibliography of Social Sciences* (IBSS);
- *Social Sciences Citation Index*.

Journal publishers' websites Publishers have developed more sophisticated indexes and search facilities on their websites, which can be a useful way to locate journal articles. Often these websites have alerting services for their journals so you can have email alerts sent to you when new issues of your favourite journals are published.

There are two major alerting services for the UK: ZETOC (http://zetoc.jisc.ac.uk) is an electronic table of contents service based on the holdings of the British Library; and JournalTOCs (http://www.journaltocs.ac.uk), hosted at Heriot Watt University, claims to be the biggest free table of contents service. These are useful services for keeping track of what is being published in the journals of your choice.

Citation of articles

Articles in legal journals may be cited in abbreviated form:

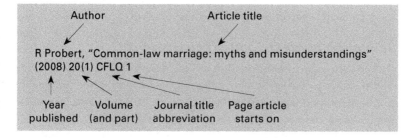

NB There is some variation in both this style of citation and in the abbreviations used for journal titles.

Or with journal title in full:

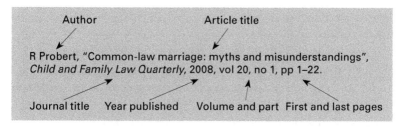

The particular form of citation depends on the house style of the publisher or institution.

How to find articles by citation

Identifying abbreviations   If given a full citation, it is likely the only information you will lack is which journal the abbreviation refers to. This can be discovered by using traditional and online sources. Once you have deciphered the abbreviation:

- check online sources available to you for the full-text journal; or
- check library catalogues to find the printed journal and locate the article by volume, part and page number.

Traditional   Abbreviations may be checked in a variety of print sources. These include the table of abbreviations in the *Current Law Year Book* and *Monthly Digest*. D Raistrick, *Index to Legal Citations and Abbreviations* (3rd edn, 2008) also includes abbreviations from law reports and sources from non-UK jurisdictions.

Online   The *Cardiff Index to Legal Abbreviations* (http://www.legalabbrevs. cardiff.ac.uk/) allows you to search for the full title from of an abbreviation, or to find the preferred abbreviation for a full title. The service also covers law reports and sources from non-UK jurisdictions.

How to find articles by author and/or title

Online indexes are sophisticated so it is often possible to find articles even with the most partial or sketchy information. However, given the amount of information online, it is useful to have as much information as possible and to know the best place to look. If you have the title of the article you want, it is very likely that you will be able to find it via a number of routes. Having only the author is a bit trickier as there can be two people with the same or very similar names, and author names can be indexed in different ways.

Web search engine   You could use a web search engine and look for the article by putting the article title between quotation marks ". . .". This is called a phrase search (see Chapter 10 for tips on effective searching). This should retrieve the article details and you will be able to open the full text if your institution/library has a subscription (you will normally need to log in).

Web-scale discovery services   These are common services now in libraries and large institutions. They offer powerful searches across large amounts of licensed (subscribed) data and owned content (ebooks, ejournals, theses, newspapers, etc). Common examples are Summon, Primo and Ebsco Discovery Service. Advanced search features allow searching by author but you can do a general search for the author and words from the title to find journal articles (and other material) matching your terms.

Westlaw   In the "Journals" search screen, enter the author name(s) in the "Author" field and/or keywords from the title in the "Article Title" field. If the journal is indexed in *Westlaw*, results will contain details of where the article is published. A link to the full text of the article is provided if it is available on *Westlaw*.

Lexis®Library   The "Journals" search screen allows you to enter terms in the "Author" and "Article Title" fields. It retrieves "UK Journals Index" summaries and the full-text articles available on *Lexis®Library*.

Lawtel   A Lawtel UK "Articles Index" search permits entry of terms in the "Author" and "Title" fields. Results give publication details for articles.

JustCite The "Articles" search screen allows entry of terms in the "Title" field. Results provide article publication details with links to available sources for the full-text document.

How to find articles by subject

Online subscription services make searching for articles on a subject easy. The *Current Law Monthly Digest* lists articles published each month under subject headings.

Web-scale discovery services These services are designed for easy, effective keyword searching. They use complex algorithms to make sure that results are ranked by relevance, ie that you find articles matching your search. The trick is to get the keywords or concepts right (see Chapter 10 for tips and a fuller discussion on keywords). These work very well for searching for articles by subject.

Online subscriptions services

Westlaw The "Journals" basic search allows entry of terms in the "free text" search field. The advanced search also provides a search field for "Subject/Keyword". When using the "Subject/Keyword" field, terms should be chosen carefully; to assist with this, there is a link to a "list of terms" which have been used in indexing and reflect the content in the database.

Lexis®Library The "Journals" search allows entry of terms in a general search field and also has the option of adding indexed subject terms (or "topics") to a search.

Lawtel The "Articles Index" search allows entry of terms in "Free Text", "Subject" and "Keywords" search fields.

JustCite The "Articles" search screen allows entry of terms in "Subject" and "Abstract" fields. Results provide article publication details with links to available sources for the full-text document.

NB When searching *Westlaw, Lexis®Library*, and other database services which contain the full text of articles, it is important to be aware that "free text" searches will look for words occurring anywhere in an article. Careful use of terms and connectors is important in such searches. See Chapter 10 for a fuller discussion of connectors and search operators.

Other ways to find articles

Westlaw's "Journals" advanced search provides options for specifying case law and legislation referred to in an article. (Similar options are available in *Lawtel*'s "Article Index" search.) References to relevant articles are also given in *Westlaw*'s "Case Analysis" and "Legislation Analysis" documents retrieved through "Cases" and "Legislation" searches.

Use the information that you have. It can be very tempting to keep searching but it is important to fully use the sources you already have. As has been indicated elsewhere, you should use the footnotes and bibliography to note other relevant literature.

Online databases because they are hyperlinked also allow you to move from a record to other material by the same author (by clicking on the hyperlink of their name) or on a similar topic (by clicking on the subject headings). Sometimes you can also link directly to the full text of material which is cited in footnotes or in a reference list or bibliography at the end of the work.

OTHER SECONDARY SOURCES

Theses

A thesis is a piece of research submitted by a research student. Normally, these are long, in-depth pieces of work created over years of research. You may wish to refer to these when undertaking your own dissertation or other piece of research. It might be sufficient just to look at the abstract and the references to identify material of relevance to your own research. Theses are held by the library of the university which awarded the Ph.D. and some are now available in full online. To locate theses on a topic you can search:

- the catalogues of university libraries;
- Google Scholar (https://scholar.google.co.uk/) – indexes institutional repositories where many theses are held;
- the *Index to Theses* (http://www.theses.com/);
- *EThOS* (http://ethos.bl.uk/Home.do) – the British Library's database of digitised UK Ph.D. theses; or
- NDLTD (http://www.ndltd.org/) – Networked Digital Library of Theses and Dissertations, which you can search for non-UK theses.

Newspapers

Newspaper articles provide news of legal developments including newly decided cases and proposed legislation. Articles can provide in-depth analysis and place legal issues in their wider social context. Public, legal and statutory notices provide information relevant to practitioners' work. Sources of newspapers include:

- libraries – usually take a selection in print and may retain an archive;
- individual newspapers – have their own websites;
- *Lexis®Library*, *Proquest Newsstand* and *Nexis® UK* – provide access to a searchable archive of many UK newspapers (with appropriate subscriptions);
- *Westlaw UK*'s "Current Awareness" search and *Lawtel*'s "Articles Index" – can be used to find summaries of legal articles from some newspapers. *Westlaw*'s "News" database provides access to full-text articles from local and national newspapers (with appropriate subscriptions).

"Think-tanks" etc

Research organisations, known as "think-tanks", produce reports and other documents, which may influence government policy and legislative developments. Examples include the Institute for Public Policy Research (IPPR) and the Constitution Unit at University College London.

Similar influential documents may be produced by other bodies including trade unions, political parties, the Law Society of Scotland, and various "pressure groups".

Reports may be available from these organisations' websites or published as monographs and available in libraries.

Blogs etc

Blogs are websites which contain short commentaries and news items usually posted by a single author. Their reliability and usefulness depends on the author and what you are using a blog to find out. Like all information you should always be aware of the authority of the information (who has created it – and why). Blogs are very common and some are excellent current awareness tools, if they are done well.

Legal blogs and current awareness sites can provide news of developments in the law and may offer useful insights. Examples include:

- *Scots Law News* (http://www.law.ed.ac.uk/sln/) – hosted by the School of Law at the University of Edinburgh;
- *CaseCheck* (http://www.casecheck.co.uk/) – contains case summaries and articles posted by legal practitioners; and
- *UK Human Rights Blog* (http://ukhumanrightsblog.com/about/).

Essential Facts

- Institutional writings codified Scots law in the 17th to 19th centuries. They are considered a formal source of Scots law in the absence of other authority.
- The Law Commissions issue consultation papers and reports as part of the process of reviewing the law.
- Textbooks contain authors' statements of the law and their commentaries on it. It is important to use an up-to-date edition of a textbook. The index can help you find information within the book.
- Encyclopaedias aim to give a comprehensive account of the law in general or in a particular area. *The Laws of Scotland: Stair Memorial Encyclopaedia* and *Halsbury's Laws of England* are important works and are available via *Lexis®Library*.
- Library catalogues can be used to find print and electronic versions of books and journals.
- Journal articles provide up-to-date and detailed legal information. Journals are published in parts and are a key academic source.
- Many journals are available online and print copies may be found in libraries.
- The *Legal Journals Index* (available through the "Journals" search on *Westlaw*) is particularly useful in finding out where an article has been published.

Further Reading

- F Grant, *Legal Research Skills for Scots Lawyers* (3rd edn, 2014), Chapter 8.
- P Clinch, *Using a Law Library: a student's guide to legal research skills* (2nd edn, 2001), Chapters 8 and 13.
- J W Colquhoun, *Finding the Law: a handbook for Scots lawyers* (1999), Chapters 3, 9 and 10.
- J Knowles, *Effective Legal Research* (4th edn, 2016), Chapters 1, 5 and 7.

10 SOLVING LEGAL PROBLEMS: WRITING AND RESEARCH

FORMULATING A RESEARCH STRATEGY

Good research begins with a clear understanding of what it is you want to know. On the face of it this may seem quite obvious but by definition, at the start of a research project, you are in a state of unknowing; you are "in the dark" about certain things and need to find information (be enlightened). Articulating your information need – your "known unknowns" – is an essential first step because if you do not know what you are looking for, how do you know where to look?

Understanding what you want to know will depend on the type of question or legal problem you are trying to answer. Defining what that is involves analysing the question and identifying aims, scope, boundaries and relevant types of information. For example, are you looking at the law in a single jurisdiction or are you making a comparison? Do you need to look at Bills or draft legislation? What secondary sources are appropriate? Do you need to look at grey literature (eg government publications, organisational information) or statistical data? When you have thought about that, you can then begin to operationalise your question – that means identifying keywords and phrases that reflect your question and creating effective searches using the most appropriate tools, eg catalogue, database, search engine or website. There is no single database or search tool that will completely answer your need; instead, you are likely to use a combination of all of these. Throughout the book we have been identifying some of the key tools that you can use. Getting to know what these are good for (ie what information they contain) will make undertaking research much easier.

Finding information is only one part of the process. Of equal significance is being able to evaluate what you have found – both in terms of the process (do you need to amend your search strategy if you have not found what you were looking for, or if you have found too much?) and the information itself. Research is an iterative process; you will follow the same steps a number of times as you build up your knowledge. You look, find, evaluate, identify more questions, look, find, etc. You should also develop the practice of recording what you have found (and how you found it) and referencing sources you use in producing your work.

ANALYSING AND ANSWERING LAW QUESTIONS

Generally, there are two main forms of questions in law examinations and coursework: essay questions and problem questions. Answering these, particularly problem questions, requires certain skills. Some guidelines to help you tackle these types of question are set out below:

Essay questions

These are not essentially different from the essay questions that you will encounter in other subjects, and many of the same rules apply. As with all forms of question (particularly in exams) the first rule is to read the question carefully and make sure that you answer what has been asked. Few, if any, questions ask you to write all you know about a subject and yet this is what many students do. If you are asked to "discuss" or "explain" something or to "compare" different things, then that is what you should do. This means that sometimes a certain amount of explanation, or even critical comment is required, and not just a regurgitation of facts. The purpose of any question is to test your understanding, not just your memory.

Research required for essay questions, while requiring the use of primary sources, usually draws heavily on journal articles, background materials, and other sources discussing the law.

The wording of the question indicates the approach you should take to research.

> *Example*:
>
> "Much uncertainty surrounds the circumstances in which gender reassignment should be recognised for the purposes of marriage." (Lord Nicholls, in *Bellinger* v *Bellinger* [2003] 2 AC 467, at 478). Discuss the development of the law in this area.

Elements of this question include: recognition of gender reassignment; marriage; uncertainty surrounding when there should be recognition; the *Bellinger* case; and the law's development. The purpose of the question is given in the phrase "discuss the development ...". This indicates you should examine how the law has changed over time (and may change in the future) and look at the various reasons for this as well as the changes' impact. The question suggests that you would need to look at primary materials, such as the *Bellinger* case itself, and also secondary sources such as textbooks and journals to find the opinions of commentators.

Problem questions

Mere regurgitation of facts is even more fatal in the case of problem questions. These are very common in law and you will not be able to avoid them. This is because problem questions are the best way to test the legal skills needed to apply the law in real life. If you consult a lawyer, it is not enough for him or her simply to know the law. He or she needs to be able to identify the legal rules that should be applied to your particular problem in order to solve it. Not only that, but if your case goes to court, he or she will have to back up their arguments with relevant legal authority in the form of statute or case law. Even if it does not go to court, the use of authority can be used to convince an opponent to seek an out-of-court settlement. Problem questions test your skill by setting out a hypothetical case which will usually require you to apply several different legal rules or principles. Your task is to pick out the correct rules and apply them to the problem with reference to legal authority where appropriate.

Problem questions may require research to determine the relevant law. You are usually concerned only with finding the law as it stands now (or at a specific date).

Specimen problem question (law of contract)

> Mary Hill is employed as a private nurse for the ageing millionaire, Lord Lucre. Using her considerable powers of charm and persuasion, she gets him to sell her an old painting from his private gallery for £100. She does not tell him any lies, but he gets the impression that she wants to keep it for herself. Lord Lucre is still of reasonably sound mind, though he is no longer as sharp as he was in his youth.
>
> Mary immediately sells the painting to Lovejob, a dealer, for £500. Lovejob knows that the painting belongs to the French Depressionist School and is worth much more. However, he says nothing of this to Mary and resells the painting to the private collector, Kelvin Grove, for £10,000. Both Lovejob and Kelvin believe that this fairly represents the value of the painting.
>
> It now turns out that the painting is a genuine Potboiller worth half a million pounds. Lord Lucre, Mary, Lovejob and Kelvin Grove are claiming ownership of it. Examine the validity of the various contracts in order to determine the true owner.

Specimen answer

> To answer this question, we must examine the validity of three contracts, ie those between (1) Lord Lucre and Mary; (2) Mary and Lovejob; and (3) Lovejob and Kelvin Grove.

In the case of the contract between Lord Lucre and Mary Hill, there are two possible grounds of challenge – (a) facility and circumvention and (b) undue influence. Facility is a weakness of mind falling short of insanity and circumvention is a motive to mislead falling short of fraud. Neither of these on its own affects the validity of a contract, but a combination of the two may make a contract voidable. We are told that Lord Lucre is still of reasonably sound mind, though not as sharp as in his youth; this suggests that he has not lost his contractual capacity through insanity, but that his mind may have been sufficiently weakened by age for him to be described as facile. There is no indication that Mary has been fraudulent (she told no lies), but the false impression gained by Lord Lucre about her intentions regarding the painting suggests that she may have had a motive to mislead. There is therefore a good case for arguing that there has been facility and circumvention.

Also, Mary has abused the position of trust between nurse and patient in order to induce Lord Lucre into a bad bargain, and there is no indication that he has had the benefit of independent advice. This suggests that there may have been undue influence, which could also make the contract voidable.

However, since the contract was at the most voidable (ie valid until challenged), it was valid at the time of the sale to Lovejob. Mary has therefore provisionally obtained ownership at this stage.

In the contract between Mary and Lovejob, there has been a failure on the part of Lovejob to disclose a material fact; namely that the painting is much more valuable than Mary realises. We are not dealing with a contract *uberrimae fidei*, nor is there a fiduciary relationship between Mary and Lovejob, either of which would have created a duty of disclosure. We are therefore left with the general rule that, in the absence of fraud, there is no obligation on either party to disclose a material fact which is unknown to the other and which might influence his or her decision on whether or not to enter the contract. The parties are said to be "at arms length", and it is up to each of them to discover any material facts for themselves. This principle is illustrated by the case of *Gillespie* v *Russel* (1853) where a tenant entering in a mineral lease knew that the mine contained a particularly valuable seam of minerals, a fact unknown to the other party. It was held that the contract was valid: there had been no fraud, merely failure to disclose a material fact.

As the second contract is therefore valid, ownership has passed at this stage from Mary to Lovejob. This means that, even if the first contract was indeed voidable, it can no longer be challenged, since a third party (namely Lovejob) has now obtained a real right of ownership in the painting.

The ground of challenge to be considered in relation to the third contract is that Lovejob and Kelvin Grove made a common error (ie the same error) about the value of the painting. A common error as to a material fact may make a contract void, but where the common error relates only to a matter of value or opinion, the contract's validity is unaffected. A case in point is *Dawson* v *Muir* where vats sunk in the ground were sold for £2, a price which both parties believed reflected their true value. The vats were later found to contain white lead worth £300, but it was held that this did not make the contract open to challenge.

Since the third contract is also valid, Kelvin Grove is the owner of the painting.

Points to note

The following observations apply mainly to problem questions, but some are also relevant to essay questions:

- Keep to the point and only refer to areas of law which are relevant to the problem set. In the above example, the relevant ones are Facility and Circumvention, Undue Influence, Failure to Disclose a Material Fact, and Common Error as to a matter of value or opinion. In a problem question, a general discussion on the law of contract will earn no marks and may even lose you some, if you get some of the irrelevant material wrong. The less you say the better chance you have of concealing your weaknesses.

- Read the question carefully. Most of what you are told is there for a reason and probably has some legal significance. If you have only identified one or two relevant areas of law, then you may be missing something.

- In a court, there are two types of issue to be resolved: questions of fact, which are proved (or otherwise) by evidence; and questions of law, which are settled by legal debate. In problem questions you are only concerned with questions of law: you can assume that the facts given in the question could be proved in court.

- When quoting cases, you do not need to state the facts at great length. While you will get credit for correctly quoting a case, what you get most marks for is identifying and stating the relevant legal principles. However, knowing cases will help to steer you in the right direction, as problem questions will often resemble cases you have learned. In the specimen question, the fact that Lovejob, a buyer, knew something important that the seller did not and kept his mouth shut about it, may remind you of the situation in *Gillespie* v *Russel*. If you also remember that the case concerned failure to disclose a material fact, then you have identified the principle you are looking for. You may be able to do this without knowing the case, and still get the credit, but you are in more danger of going off in the wrong direction.

• Very often the answer to a problem question will be clear, particularly if there is a case directly in point. However sometimes, as in real life, it may not be possible to give a definite answer. This does not matter: what you get the marks for is identifying the issues, describing the relevant legal principles and stating the different possibilities with reference to legal authority.

• One useful rule of thumb for structuring the answers to problem questions is the ISAS formula:

> **I**DENTIFY the **AREAS of LAW** concerned
>
> **S**TATE the **LEGAL PRINCIPLES**
>
> **A**PPLY the legal principles
>
> **S**UPPORT with **AUTHORITY** (case law and/or legislation).

For example, in relation to the last point in the specimen question:

> **AREA OF LAW**:
> Contract; validity of contracts; common error.
>
> **LEGAL PRINCIPLE**:
> Common error as to a matter of value or opinion does not make a contract invalid.
>
> **APPLICATION**:
> The contract between Lovejob and Kelvin Grove is valid.
>
> **AUTHORITY**:
> *Dawson* v *Muir*.

SELECTING SEARCH TERMS

As we said earlier, first you need to know what you are looking for. Having identified the type of information you need, the next step is to list keywords and subject terms that reflect that. Online tools like databases, search engines and websites work by matching keywords against the information they contain, so getting those keywords right is important. You will have some idea of relevant words which describe what you are looking for but you should take time to identify **broader, narrower** and **related terms, synonyms (alternative terms)** and **antonyms (opposite terms)**. This is because databases contain literature from diverse sources reflecting different disciplines, individuals who express themselves differently, international literature, subject-specific terminology, etc. If you only use very limited keywords, you may miss lots of relevant and useful literature.

The following example, for the term "marriage", illustrates how many search terms may be used in the literature:

Original term	Broader terms	Narrower terms	Related terms	Synonyms (alternatives)	Antonyms (opposites)
Marriage	Relationships Family law	Spouse Husband Wife	Wedding Civil partnership Cohabitation Succession Property Children Parents	Matrimony Nuptial Conjugal	Divorce Separation Annulment

How do you identify keywords? The first place to start is with your existing knowledge. You will already know something about the subject. Write down all the relevant words you can think of. You could use a legal dictionary, thesaurus or some key textbooks to help identify more. A good way to generate keywords is to search for some literature on a database or search engine (we discussed some of these in the previous chapter – Summon, Primo or Ebsco Discovery). You can use the results to pick up other relevant keywords from journal article titles, abstracts and keywords or subject headings assigned to the articles by the author or indexer.

When selecting terms, be aware that terminology can vary between jurisdiction and over time. For example, Scots law uses the terms "delict" and "servitude" where English law uses "tort" and "easement" to express similar concepts. In the past, "law of master and servant" was used to refer to what we now call "employment law".

SEARCH SYSTEMATICALLY

Where to begin

Lecture notes   At university you will have access to lecture notes and reading lists of relevant reading materials.

Textbooks   In addition to books your lecturer has recommended on reading lists, use a library catalogue to identify other books on your topic. Remember that because library catalogues index information about books rather than the whole book (as a database or search engine might), you may need to use broader search terms to find relevant books. When you have some textbooks, use the index and table of contents in each to identify the most relevant sections. You might use these for background or overviews of a subject and to identify keywords, authors and other literature (from the content itself or in footnotes or the bibliography).

Encyclopaedias   An encyclopaedia like the *Stair Memorial Encyclopaedia* can be a really useful way to get an expert overview of a topic as well as identifying key authorities. Alternatively, use a library catalogue to identify a specialist encyclopaedia in the area you are researching. Use the index (or online search options) to find relevant sections.

Follow up references

Remember, research is not a linear process; it is continuous. So you are using what you find not only for the arguments and theories of that author but also to identify other works referred to and discussed. This is true throughout the research process but is especially useful at the early stages when you are finding your way through the literature. So use what you find to follow up the references. These might include: cases, legislation, journal articles, books, official publications, theses, etc.

Search online sources

Search all relevant services to which you have access and which you have identified as appropriate. This will be a mix of subscription databases, search engines and freely accessible websites. Each will have merit in terms of its features and content. Databases all have some content that is unique and all will have overlap. Which you choose will depend on exactly what you need at that stage of your research.

As we have noted, the key thing is to know what you are looking for. When you do, it is much easier to know which is the best tool for that particular job. So, if you need to know about how a piece of legislation has been considered in the courts, you might use *Westlaw*, *Lexis®Library* or a traditional (print) law citator. If, however, you wanted to find academic articles, you might use a legal database, a larger multi-disciplinary database, a search engine or a publisher's website. The most effective searches will depend on what information you have and the search facilities in each of these tools. You need to be able to adapt your technique accordingly.

Update/trace back

Update   Whatever source you use, it is important for legal arguments that you are using the current law. Check appropriate resources for any recent changes in case law and legislation. You may also wish to check whether there are any pending changes (eg Bills currently in progress).

Trace back   Use online and print resources to trace past developments in case law and legislation.

A good search involves moving between different types of source. Use everything at your disposal and think of sources in terms of all their constituent parts. Make use of indexes, tables of cases and statutes, footnotes, and bibliographies, which are all useful to the researcher.

Effective online searching

Online databases and search engines have features which allow for different approaches to searching, including usually a basic search where you enter keywords in a single search box, to more advanced search options. Although not all databases share the same features, there are some general principles which you can apply across different tools.

Boolean searching

"Boolean" and other search operators are common across most databases and search engines. They are used to connect search terms in a logical way to broaden (expand) or narrow (focus) the search. Common search operators include:

- *AND* – narrows your search as it restricts results to documents containing **both** terms. Eg the search *marriage AND transgender* should retrieve **fewer** results than a search using *marriage* alone. When you search using more than one keyword, a database or search engine will assume an AND between terms (so the more terms you use, the narrower the search). Variations include & and +.
- *OR* – broadens your search as it expands results to documents containing **either** term. Eg the search *marriage OR matrimonial* should retrieve **more** results than a search using *marriage* alone. This is particularly useful for synonyms, related terms and abbreviations.
- *NOT* – restricts results to documents containing the first term **but not** the second. Eg the search *marriage NOT succession* should retrieve **fewer** results than a search using *marriage* alone. Variations include BUT NOT, AND NOT.

- *"Near" or "proximity" operators* – indicate the distance between search terms, which is a useful way to focus a search for terms that are not a phrase but are likely to be in proximity to one another in a document. You can restrict results to those containing the terms within a given number of words of each other or within the same sentence or paragraph. Variations include:
  - */n* (on *Westlaw*) and *w/n* (on *Lexis®Library*) – search for terms occurring within a given number of words of each other: eg *marriage /5 transgender* retrieves documents where the terms occur within 5 words of each other.
  - */s* and *w/s* – search for terms occurring in the same sentence: eg *marriage /s transgender*.
  - */p* and *w/p* – search for terms occurring in the same paragraph: eg *marriage /p transgender*.

- *Phrases* – placing quotation marks " " round terms restricts results to documents with that exact phrase. Eg *"civil partnership"* retrieves documents containing this phrase where a search for *civil AND partnership* will retrieve documents with both words appearing anywhere in the document, together in a phrase or not.

- *"Truncation" (eg *)* – expands results to retrieve documents containing terms with a common "root". Eg *cohabit** would retrieve documents containing *cohabit, cohabitation, cohabitant,* and *cohabiting.* Variations include ! , ? and *.

- *"Wildcard" (eg ?)* – expands results by retrieving documents containing spelling variations or related words. Eg the search *ombudsm?n* retrieves documents containing *ombudsman* and *ombudsmen.* Variations include * and #.

- *Parentheses/brackets ( )* – organise and group terms. Eg a search (*marriage OR "civil partnership") AND (transgender OR transsexual)* looks for documents containing either terms *marriage* or *civil partnership* and then looks for those documents which also contain either *transgender* or *transsexual.* This allows you to control complex searches which contain several terms.

NB Different databases use different symbols for the same connector. Databases' "Help" sections will explain how to use connectors.

Fields

Another common way to focus your search is to use "fields". This means matching search terms against certain parts of a record so you can limit a search by specifying the "field" in which terms occur. Categories of field depend on the database and type of document: a "journals" search might include *Author, Title, Abstract* and *Full Text* fields; a "cases" search might include *Party Names, Court, Judge* and *Headnote* fields.

You can usually do this on an "advanced search" screen. Do not let that terminology put you off. You do not need to be an expert searcher to use an "advanced search", and very often these are much easier to use than the basic search screen as you are guided to enter terms in appropriate fields. Search operators (discussed above) are often embedded in "advanced search" screens making them easy and intuitive to use.

Date

Most search engines and databases have a date filter which allows you to specify the date range of the material you want to find. It is also possible on online databases and search tools to have graphics which show the amount of literature published within each year. This can be useful to spot patterns in the literature (eg when there was increased interest in a specific area).

Coverage

You should be aware of the information covered by databases. This will help you decide which database is best for your particular search. For example, you will not find a journal article if searching a database which contains only cases. Other important considerations include: the dates of coverage (how far back in time or how current the content is); jurisdictions; individual journals indexed; and the availability of full-text documents.

Information about coverage is usually found within database services by following links to "coverage", "content", "information", "about" etc but you will build up this knowledge as you use databases and online services.

EVALUATE SOURCES

It is your decision to decide which sources are relevant and appropriate for your research. This is particularly important if you are using a search engine to find material as there are so many different types of information from different sources indexed, so you need to be conscious of exactly what you are looking at. There are some key criteria you can use to evaluate information:

Who?

- *Author* Who has written the document? What expertise or authority do they have in the subject? What else have they written? It is useful, for example, to look at the author affiliation when you are using a journal article. The author affiliation is normally given under the author name, under the journal abstract or beside other information about the article. This will tell you if the author is an academic and if so, where they are based. This is useful if you want to contact the author or just to check what else they have written (or if they are currently working on any research as this may be mentioned on the institution website). The author might be a practitioner rather than an academic, so that will give you a different viewpoint. Who the author is provides some context for the work. Understanding the authority of the literature does not necessarily mean that you consider one author to be more worthy than another (although that could be the case), but that you, as the researcher, understand the context of the information.

- *Publisher.* Who has published the document? Are they a well-known legal or academic publisher? Are they a recognised institution? Is it "self-published" (eg on a private website)? Does an article appear in a peer-reviewed journal? Again, this consideration is to provide some context for the information that you are evaluating. In an online environment, it is often the case that the author and the publisher are the same (particularly for corporate information). Information is created and distributed now in far more spaces and much more quickly than ever before so understanding its provenance is vital to the researcher.

When?

- *Date* When was the document created? Is information likely to be out of date? Are there more recent versions (eg updates, new editions) available? Has the law changed since publication? In terms of the scope of your research, is the material within an appropriate date range? How does the work relate to other literature you have found in terms of currency and context?

Where?

- *Jurisdiction* Where was the document written? To which legal systems does it apply? If it is a UK text, does it take account of differences between Scots and English law? This is important particularly when you are using a search engine rather than a legal database.

Why?

Purpose

Why was the document written? What is its purpose and who is the intended audience? Does the author or publisher have a vested interest in the topic? Is any bias declared? For material that you find online, it is important to make this consideration. Again, this helps you to put the material in context and to decide on its validity and relevance to your research.

What?

- *Relevance* Is the subject relevant to your research topic?
- *Accuracy* Is the text well researched? Are references given to texts supporting the writer's arguments? Are you able to verify the accuracy of supporting evidence? What methodology did the writer use? If the material is online, are the links broken? Has the site been updated recently?
- *Criticism* For journal articles and other academic sources, you might also want to think about how that article has been received since it was published, ie what impact did it make? You can track this using citation data. Google Scholar (https://scholar.google.co.uk/) is a useful tool for this. Citation data (shown as a "*Cited by*" link) is usually indicated under the brief record for articles. Click on that to see the journals and other literature that have cited the work. You can look at citation data by year, which can be useful when there is a lot of it and also to see if older works are still being cited.

Online evaluation

Evaluation is necessary whatever the medium of the material as it is important to place information in an academic and social context. However, special care must be taken when evaluating information found on the web – especially if this has been found using a general search engine. Given the increase of freely available quality legal sources on the web and the use of search engines to locate these, there can be a dependence on web search engines as the tool of choice for research and an assumption that information sources found in this way have equal value. General search engines (unlike subscription services) have massive indexes of information of varying quality which is not organised or structured. Responsibility for assessing the validity or relevance of information found in this way lies solely with the researcher. Therefore, you must apply evaluation criteria diligently.

RECORDING

Why record?

By keeping a record, you remain in control of the research process, which will give you confidence as you proceed. It will be your choice how you manage this but you could keep records which might show the sources you have already found, those which you have read, and those for which you have references but have yet to locate. In this way, you avoid retreading the same ground or missing sources you intended to use. An accurate research record also makes compiling references and a bibliography easier at a later stage.

What to record

You need to record information which allows you to locate the source in the future. It is advisable to record it in the form you would use to cite the source in your footnotes and bibliography, which just makes it all much easier when you are ready to submit the final piece of work.

It's also useful to keep a note of the resources you used in your research (eg library catalogues, online databases, etc) and the searches you performed. This might seem unnecessary but it can save you time when you are conducting a long piece of work (like a dissertation or other long research project). Lists of keywords, subject terms, authors and key sources are useful throughout your research. You will not include this information in your final work, but it will help keep you on track.

How to record

You could create an "evidence table" (using a spreadsheet or table) to record the sources you use and their significance for your research. Categories you record might include author, title, source, date, main arguments, strengths and weaknesses. This can help provide an overall picture of the sources you have found. If you have access to "reference management" software (eg *EndNote* or *Refworks*), you can use this as it will have features for storing and managing references and documents. Your method of recording and storing information should be flexible and allow you to sort and reorder references required.

REFERENCING

You should always provide accurate references to the sources which you have used directly in your own work. In addition you should provide a bibliography of all materials used in the preparation of your work, even if you have not drawn on these directly in the final piece.

There are a number of reasons for doing this: to provide authority for your arguments, to show the breadth and depth of your research, to help your reader locate the sources of your arguments and to avoid accusations of plagiarism.

Authority

When stating the law, you should make reference to relevant case law, legislation or other legal authority. Be as precise as possible: eg identify the relevant provision of legislation, or indicate the *ratio decidendi* of a case.

When making arguments in an essay, you should cite the work of other authors to support these (as appropriate) or provide a contrary opinion. When giving statistical or other evidence, or giving examples, these too should be accurately referenced.

By providing appropriate references, you demonstrate that you have properly researched your work and strengthen the arguments you make.

Plagiarism

Plagiarism is the process of using the work of another person and presenting it as your own. It is the result of failing to sufficiently acknowledge the use you have made of the ideas or words of others. Plagiarism can be deliberate, where you knowingly copy another's work and pass it off as your own; or it can be inadvertent, where you simlify fail to provide a reference.

To avoid plagiarising another's work, acknowledge all sources you use. Even if you use your own words to describe another's ideas (paraphrasing), you should acknowledge the source. If you use the exact words of an author, place these in quotation marks and acknowledge the source. **If in doubt, acknowledge the source.**

Referencing systems

There are several referencing systems that you can use. Which one you choose may depend on the "house style" of your law school. Above all, once you have selected a system use it consistently – do not mix different systems in the same piece of work as this is confusing and aggravating for your reader.

Common referencing systems include:

- *Footnotes/Oxford referencing*: this uses a system of superscript numbers in the text referring to numbered notes at the foot of the page.

- *Name and date/the "Harvard" system*: this uses a reference within the text to indicate the author and publication year of the source cited and, if appropriate, the page number:

> The Government believes that the Supreme Court will enhance judicial independence (McFadzean, 2007, p 29).

or

> McFadzean (2007, p 29) notes that the Government believes the Supreme Court will enhance judicial independence.

The works referred to are then listed at the end of the work in a list of references or bibliography.

- *Numeric system*: this system numbers sources according to the order in which they are cited in the text. For example, the third source cited is numbered [3] and referred to by this number if it is cited later in the text. The works referred to are then listed at the end of the text in numerical order.
- *Harvard Law Review Association/The Blue Book*: this system is used primarily in the United States. It is best explained in Harvard Law Review Association, *The Bluebook: A Uniform System of Citation* (20th edn, 2015).

Form of references

Throughout this book examples have been given of how different materials might be cited. This is helpful in being able to identify what you are looking at (eg a book, or chapter, or journal article, or official document, etc). While general principles apply to the referencing of some materials, the precise details of how a particular type of source should be referenced can vary. Different methods of referencing can be equally valid; pick one and stick with it.

Your principal source of guidance on the form of references should be any "style sheet" produced by your law school. This will contain the department's house style including details of any preferred referencing system and the form references and bibliographies should take. In the absence of any house style, or on points where there is no guidance, the following works may help:

- S Meredith and D Nolan, *OSCOLA: The Oxford University Standard for the Citation of Legal Authorities* (available via URL: https://www.law. ox.ac.uk/research-subject-groups/publications/oscola);

- F Grant, *Legal Research Skills for Scots Lawyers* (3rd edn, 2014), Chapter 13;
- D French, *How to Cite Legal Authorities* (1996);
- R Pears and G Shields, *Cite them Right: the essential referencing guide* (9th edn, 2013).

Referencing online sources

If referencing a source only available online (ie "born digital") then you should cite the online source (guidance should be given in your department's style sheet or in the works mentioned above).

However, if a source is available both online and in print, it is preferable to refer to the printed source (even if, in fact, you accessed an online version).

Moreover, you should not refer to the online database which you used to access a case, legislation, journal article, etc. Instead, you should refer to the content – case, legislation, or journal article – as if you had accessed it in print.

Bibliographies

A bibliography should give details of all materials used in preparing your work even if you have not drawn on these directly in the final piece. The style and format of your bibliography should conform to any house style. The texts, referred to above, which offer guidance on form of referencing, also assist in preparing bibliographies.

If you maintain an accurate record of the sources used, the preparation of your bibliography should be much easier. If you have access to "reference management" software (eg *Endnote* or *Refworks*) then this can also make creating your bibliography easier.

Essential Facts

- At the beginning of the research process, you should take time to formulate a research strategy.
- The research process should start with analysing the question and selecting appropriate search terms.
- Get an overview of a topic from a textbook or encyclopaedia before following up refer-ences, searching online databases and bringing your research up to date.
- Online searching is more effective if you use appropriate operators, fields, and date restrictions as appropriate. You should be aware of the content of the services you search.

- Evaluate the sources you find and judge whether they are reliable and relevant to your research topic.
- Recording sources as you proceed makes the research process more efficient and effective.
- Acknowledge the sources you use in references/footnotes and a bibliography. This adds strength to your arguments and avoids inadvertent plagiarism.

Further Reading

- F Grant, *Legal Research Skills for Scots Lawyers* (3rd edn, 2014) Chapters 2, 12, 13, and 14.
- E Finch and S Fafinski, *Legal Skills* (5th edn, 2015), Chapters 10–12.
- D French, *How to Cite Legal Authorities* (1996).
- R Pears and G Shields, *Cite them Right: the essential referencing guide* (9th edn, 2013).

Online Resources

- OSCOLA (https://www.law.ox.ac.uk/research-subject-groups/publications/oscola).

INDEX

Textbook titles are in italics, online sources are not.